HD
Heirs of Destiny

Being Black and God's Elect

A revealing expository on the Holy Bible in relation to the Black man and our present generation

E. Stephen Roberts

BEING BLACK and GOD'S ELECT

E. STEPHEN ROBERTS

LIVING IMAGE PUBLISHING
Chicago, Illinois

www.livingimage.org

Copyright © 2014 by E. Stephen Roberts
All rights reserved,
including the right of reproduction
in whole or in part in any form

LIVING IMAGE PUBLISHING is the authorized distributor of this book

For information regarding special discounts for bulk purchases,
please contact LIVING IMAGE PUBLISHING LLC
Tel. 1-877-462-5468
e-mail admin@livingimage.org
Internet www.livingimage.org

Logo/Branding - Charles Reese
Cover Design - Katheryn Roberts/Rebekah Roberts

Manufactured in the United States of America

10 9 8 7 6 5 4 3 2 1

Library of Congress Cataloging-in-Progress Data is available

ISBN 978-0-9818732-0-6

To contact E. Stephen Roberts visit the Heirs Of Destiny website at:
www.heirsofdestiny.com

Dedications

To my wife Katheryn,
For your most endearing spirit of love and patience, and for the many years of your tolerant gentleness throughout my personal incessant quest for truth and light. Thank you, you've made this long and demanding journey a joyful trek for my soul. I am glad that we can take this journey together, without you it would not be nearly as rewarding.

To the clergy, leaders and congregation of the Garfield Park Community Worship Center. Your faith and trust in me is humbling. To live among you is an undeniable honor, to serve you as a representative of the Kingdom of God is a genuine privilege. I thank God for you in your dedication and commitment to learning and growing in the truth.

To GOD our heavenly FATHER, without whom this treatise would be possible. Thank you for your spirit of revelation and instruction, and for your spirit of encouragement to me. Had it not been that your purposeful HAND was upon me, to guide me in every step of the way I would have not been able to stay the course. You are my LIFE and my Inspiration. Be GLORIFIED in your children for all Eternity.

E. Stephen Roberts

FOREWORD

"The voice of one crying in the wilderness, Prepare ye the way for the Lord, make straight paths." Mark 1:3

The Body of Christ is blessed to have Pastor E. Stephen Roberts as one of its powerful voices crying out in the wilderness. As a pastor, historian, and theologian, he is at the forefront of a move of God that is designed to advance divine purposes and realign life's order. His prophetic voice expressed in the pages of this book, Heirs of Destiny, is timely and relevant for a people of God who desire to experience His best and for a community who needs spiritual direction and hope.

Ingeniously, this book skillfully combines revelation with relevancy; purpose with practical application; and Christ-centeredness with cultural heritage. Such a literary approach equips the reader with biblical truths, cultural enlightenment, and life application directives for a brighter future filled with God's glory being revealed.

Heirs of Destiny can be a source of enlightenment to all but especially to African Americans and all people of African descent. Because of the evil moments of slavery and racism in North America and abroad, many would think it's folly to imagine that it was from Egypt and the black priests that emerged the birthplace of spiritual teachers. From Imhotep, the first pyramid builder, to Moses, all the way up to the followers of Jesus, their teachings are evident, although often ignored by traditional theologians.

This book lifts the spirit of *Isaiah 19:19-20*, *"In that day shall there be an altar to the Lord in the midst of the land of Egypt, and a pillar at the border thereof to the Lord. And it shall be for a sign and for a witness unto the Lord of hosts **in the land of Egypt**: for they shall cry unto the Lord because of the oppressors, and he shall send them a saviour, and a great one, and he shall deliver them."* And *Hosea 11:1*, *"When Israel was a child, then I loved him, and **called my son out of Egypt**."* And *Matthew 2:15*, *"And was there until the death of Herod: that it might be fulfilled which was spoken of the Lord by the prophet, saying, **Out of Egypt have I called my son**."* Of course the referred son in these scriptures is the blessed Son of God, Jesus the Christ. It's Him who comes out of Africa to be Savior to the lost and oppressed.

Pastor Roberts in Heirs of Destiny raises the consciousness and spirit of a people who too long have been made to feel less than a valuable contributor to the world, biblical antiquity, and the Kingdom of God. As Heirs of Destiny we cannot let the history of the European Slave Trade, segregation, Jim Crow, the New Jim Crow, racism, poverty, and the current Prison Industrial Complex, alienate us from embracing God's power and being true to His calling. It is our time to lead the world in matters of life and faith.

Pastor Roberts in Heirs of Destiny expresses the importance of knowing that Christian believers are 'heaven's treasure in earthen vessels';

"But we have this treasure in earthen vessels, that the excellency of the power may be of God, and not of us." (2nd Corinthians 4:7)

What is this treasure that we possess? This is an important question that begs answering. Within our earthen, mortal, corruptible bodies, our vile houses of clay, we possess heaven's treasure-that is, redemption in the blood of Jesus; the forgiveness of sins; a peace that surpasses all understanding; the love of God shed abroad in our hearts; the beloved powerful Spirit of God; and the image of His Son Jesus.

These attributes, along with many others, are gifts from God to help us align with His plan and purpose for our lives.

They help us find and fulfill the destiny that each has been assigned according to the will of God. But if we get stuck focusing on the poverty of life and remain impoverished in spirit, then Satan will continue to have an advantage in our churches and community. Heirs of Destiny continuously points us toward God's direction so that His glory will radiate in us and through us.

Oftentimes its hard to imagine a system of order when we live in a time where there is so much disorder, chaos, lawlessness, and rebellion in the world. However, Heirs of Destiny reminds us that Almighty God is in control and that He has an orderly plan (dispensations) for the fulfillment of His divine will. It's Him who holds the blueprint to the big picture for our individual lives and the human existence overall.

Pastor Roberts writes about the *heavenly clock of God* that we all should heed to and manage accordingly. To miss God's timing is to miss the whole thing that God purposes to do and whom He will use to do it through. Our people need to know what time it is according to God's order of things. Time has come and calls for us to get our house in order. Our natural house, our spiritual house, our physical house, our emotional house, and yes, even the church house.

God has a remarkable purpose for us *today* as we press forward as children of destiny. I implore you to study what pastor is sharing in this book. It's timely, prophetic, and necessary for such a season as this.

Heirs of Destiny: Being Black and God's Elect, comes at a time when we need a resurrection among the people of faith and the African American community. Where there exists paths of destruction, the path of destiny needs to replace it. We have in many ways fallen asleep and certain things of God has passed us by. But now is the time to arise! It's our time to advance the purposes of God, fulfill the plan of God, and live as the Children of Destiny whom God has made us.

Our salvation is in God alone. Our restoration resides with Jesus Christ. Our future hinges on possessing an unshakable uncompromising faith believing that God's plan for us is great, glorious, and good. He has tried us in the fire, we are being refined, and now's our time to shine as His pure gold. Thus, all the world will see His glory in us and working through us. It's time that we move as God's destiny child in the Spirit of Christ. That same Spirit that embeds in us the ability to lead, build, invent, and create greatness.

Pastor Roberts has presented us with a gift in Heirs of Destiny. This book will assist in your transformation and spiritual formation. I am asking that you progress through this book with a prayer that the Holy Spirit will speak to you with clarity, evoking a conviction that will fuel courage to not only change your own direction but be an agent of destiny change for those in our community. After completing this book you will be glad that you are on God's winning side, fulfilling His purposes with love and faith.

Thank you Pastor Roberts for giving us this gem from the depths of your soul. You have reminded us that we are God's chosen. I await the manifestation of more children of destiny who will embrace God's divine inheritance and press forward for the prize that resides in Christ Jesus. After introducing myself to you a few years ago in that humble suburban restaurant, I had no idea that the Lord would allow me time and space to share with you in this incredible journey as an Heir of Destiny. May the readers be enriched and blessed as I have been by this book. I am inspired by your faith, vision, and courage.

"Thy will be done on earth as it is in heaven."

Pastor Cy M. Fields
NEW LANDMARK MB CHURCH
Chicago, IL

HEIRS OF DESTINY
BEING BLACK and GOD'S ELECT

By E. Stephen Roberts

Beginnings

Page 1

CONCEPTS AND PERCEPTION

We must learn to trust. Trust God, trust one another, and trust that the foundation for an amazing and remarkable future is being established right now in this very day that is ours as God's chosen generation of the present.

Part One

Page 9

HEAVEN'S TREASURE IN EARTHEN VESSELS

This is the spiritual quest that restores the heart and soul of Black People everywhere. And fosters peace of heart among all people of every color who will receive it, in no matter what nation they may be living upon our world.

Part Two

Page 49

GOD'S ORDERLY TRANSITION OF THE AGES

According as in the Heavens God has ordained the Dispensation in which certain peoples and nations will each lead, so too does He bring-about the Destinies of men in their Times upon the Earth, so that it is God Himself who performs His Plan through every nation of man that lives here

Part Three

Page 68

IN MY COMMUNITY

The candid reflections of a Black pastor: my community is a picture of depression, deprivation and deterioration, a perfect painting of man's failure, the perfect canvass upon which God paints with the colors of His glory

Part Four

Page 79

TO THE ELECT OF GOD

What it means to be Black, Now, Chosen by God, and living your life in the most amazing relationship of all Time

Beginnings
CONCEPTS AND PERCEPTION

We must learn to trust. Trust God, trust one another, and trust that the foundation for an amazing and remarkable future is being established right now in this very day that is ours as God's chosen generation of the present.

Around the concepts of Time and Destiny, Ages and Dispensations, Life and *Being*, revolve the most complex issues that are associated with our existence as mankind. In every generation we are spiritually changing in very progressive ways. But also, every step of the way some of us are resisting the kind, merciful and benevolent purposes of the very God who has created us. The *Being* who we have become, as created in God's own image, lives in a state of continuous transformation. Today the transforming Black man is who the words of God through the prophet Micah are speaking directly to. We should be the ones who are especially preparing ourselves in this particular Time of the Ages, for allowing the gentle hand of God begin to lovingly transform us to *lead*, as He brings all of humanity into the next stage of the higher *life* for which we all have been created:

MICAH 4:6-8
"In that day, declares the LORD, I will gather the lame; I will assemble the exiles and those I have brought to grief. I will make the lame a remnant, those driven away a strong nation. The LORD will rule over them in Mount Zion from that day and forever. As for you, O watchtower of the flock, O stronghold of the Daughter of Zion, the former dominion will be restored to you; kingship will come to the Daughter of Jerusalem." New International Version

We have before us in this day of our present generation a relevant Time in which God is transforming us now for the benefit of future generations. For the benefit of generations whose Dispensation is yet to come. It is we Black people today who can identify with those who are the driven-out, the afflicted, the outcasts, targeted, the emotionally and spiritually broken wounded and hurting. And it is our very distinct and genuine responsibility to God and to the future; that we now in our present Time, think about and consider the well-being of our coming generations.

We must resolve ourselves to the reality that God's words through the prophet Micah is His message that has been brought-forth to *us* for today. Let us not misunderstand the message from God. It is so important to our present generation, and we cannot afford to get it wrong. The prophet Micah incorporates the following prophecy into this message of God for our generation: *"As for you, O **watchtower** of the **flock**, O **stronghold** of the **Daughter of Zion**, the **former dominion** will be **restored** to you; **kingship** will come to the Daughter of Jerusalem."*

watchtower: A high place that has been built for the purposes of observation. It is a place from which can be viewed all of the lands and regions that lie spread-out beneath the broad scope of its field of vision. In the case of Micah's prophetic word here, this particular *watchtower* refers to a specific group of *people* who have been chosen by God to *be* the watchtower possessing the *broad scope* of a *spiritual* and *revealing field of vision* (in their generation) on behalf of the determinate purposes of *God* which are to the good and benefit of humanity as a whole.

flock: The gathered assembly of God's chosen people. Today they would be the many hurting and broken outcasts that are scattered among Black people everywhere. This does not in any way disregard or fail to include every person (no matter what ethnicity) who has accepted Christ as their personal Savior and Lord. It *does* however exemplify the just and righteous *plans* of God, in that He has set the Ages and Dispensations and Times in which He alone will *personally* and *uniquely* minister to *all* of mankind through a specific people of His choosing. It is *true* that God *"is not a respecter of persons"*. And it is also equally true that *in* God's plans and Times of the Ages He calls forth *"a royal priesthood, a chosen generation"*.

stronghold: These chosen people of God are themselves the *spiritually fortified position* within which (in times of hardship and uncertainty) others will find spiritual safety and care from the ravages of the Times.

Daughter of Zion*:** One of several designated terms of endearment given to the *people* who are *Israel* in reflecting their special and privileged *relationship* with God as His chosen people in the Times of their generation(s). The name Zion represents the name of the City in Heaven which is of great relevance and importance to God's chosen people. Especially in so much as *entering* Zion becomes a very *real* experience to them in their *true spiritual worship* of the living God. In other words, Zion, though it is a *city* that is both Spiritual and Eternal, can be *entered* by the believer during moments of true spiritual worship. Spiritual Zion is the heavenly place of the Messiah's throne. In Hebrews 11:8-10 we find Abraham actually looking in the promised ***land for this ***heavenly*** city: *"By faith Abraham, when called to go to a place he would later receive as his inheritance, obeyed and went, even though he did not know where he was going. By faith he made his home in the promised land like a stranger in a foreign country; he lived in tents, as did Isaac and Jacob, who were heirs with him of the same promise. For he was looking forward to the city with foundations, whose architect and builder is God."* New International Version

And again; in the book of Hebrews, we find a special reference to Moses and the chosen generation of his day. They (in the Times of *their* calling) came to *Mount Sinai*, and God placed great restrictions upon the people that they should not so much as even touch the mountain. *[cf Exodus 19:9-13]*

But since Jesus Christ has ascended and sent the Holy Spirit into our world to be *with* us, we are now privileged to come before God in the Heavenly City which is *Zion*. To that end, we see in **Hebrews 12:18-24** a scene that is very explicit in its description of what is obviously *our* chosen generation's experience that is received and enjoyed *today* through our *true spiritual worship*:

> *"You have **not** come to a mountain that can be touched and that is burning with fire; to darkness, gloom and storm; to a trumpet blast or to such a voice speaking words that those who heard it begged that no further word be spoken to them, because they could not bear what was commanded: If even an animal touches the mountain, it must be stoned. The sight was so terrifying that Moses said, 'I am trembling with fear.' But you have come to Mount **Zion**, to the **heavenly** Jerusalem, the **city of the living God**. You have come to thousands upon thousands of **angels** in **joyful assembly**, to the **church** of the **firstborn**, whose names are written in heaven. You have come to **God**, the judge of all men, to the **spirits** of **righteous** men made perfect, to **Jesus** the **mediator** of a **new** covenant, and to the sprinkled blood that speaks a better word than the blood of Abel."* New International Version

former dominion: What was this *former dominion*? And what is its meaning for our present generation today? Of course we know that *former* means: *before*, or *in the past*, or *earlier* than *now*. The word *dominion* means: *to rule*, or the *power* to rule, *to govern*, or the *territory* that is governed. It can signify a person or a government of people who exercises authority (rule) over an established civilization. When God says to us (through the prophet Micah) *"the former dominion will be restored to you"* He is reminding us of a by-gone time in our far ancient past when the Black man built and governed great civilizations. And, in the reminding, God here is also saying to us: 'your ability in ancient times wherein your fathers established great civilizations and governed them is now being <u>restored</u> to your present generation'.

restored: To *give back* something that has been *taken, lost* etc. To *return* something either *to* or *beyond* its former state of what was considered as normal for it.

kingship: The *rule* and *authority* of a king (in this case Jesus Christ) over the people and territories of His Kingdom.

A Glimpse At Who We Were

Some of the below listed historical statements are racist and derogatory to both Black people and White people alike. The point we are making is not intended to be a racial slur about any human being, period. But rather, our point here is to review the report of those persons of old who actually saw some of our ancient fathers.

"....it is in fact manifest that the Colchidians are Egyptians by race....several Egyptians told me that in their opinion the Colchidians were descended from soldiers of Sesostris. I had conjectured as much myself from two pointers, firstly because they have black skins and kinky hair." **Herodotus** *c450 BC*

"Those who are too black are cowards like, for instance, the Egyptians and Ethiopians. But those who are excessively white are also cowards as we can see from the example of women....the complexion of courage is between the two, either brown or tanned."
Aristotle *c320 BC*

In More Recent Times

"....on visiting the Sphinx, the look of it gave me the clue....beholding that head characteristically negro in all its features...." **Constantin-Francois Volney** *A.D. 1783*

"The chief source of our information concerning the doctrine of *'the resurrection'* and of *'the future life'* as held by the *'Egyptians'* is, of course, the great collection of *'religious texts'* generally known by the name of *'Book Of The Dead'*. ....these wonderful compositions cover a period of *'more than five thousand years'*, and they reflect *'faithfully'*....the *'sublime beliefs'*, and the *'high ideals'*, and *'noble aspirations'* of the Egyptians." **Egyptologist: Sir E.A. Wallis Budge**

From his book 'Egyptian Religion' Published in 1959 [italics mine]

From some of the *scrolls* of these ancient *'religious texts'* of which E.A. Wallis Budge wrote we find the following interpretations, as they were interpreted by these ancient Egyptian Black priests, to the ancient Greek philosophers and scholars who came to Egypt in order to learn from them after Alexander the Great (son of King Phillip) had invaded Africa/Egypt in 333/332 BC:

The Pre-eminence Of God
"God is one and alone, and none other exists with him."

The Pre-existence Of The God Of Creation
"God is the one, the one who has made all things."

"God is from the beginning, and he has been from the beginning; he has existed from old and was when nothing else had being. He existed when nothing else existed, he created after he had come into being. He is the father of beginnings."

"God made the universe, and he created all that therein is: he is the creator of the world, of what was, of what is, and of what shall be. He is creator of the world, and it was he who fashioned it with his hands before there was any beginning; and he established it with that which went forth from him. He is the creator of the heavens, and the earth, and the deep, and the waters, and the mountains. God has stretched out the heavens and founded the earth. What his heart conceived came to pass straightway, and when he had spoken his word came to pass; and it shall endure forever."

The Hidden Spirit and Divine Nature of God
"God is a spirit, a hidden spirit, the spirit of spirits, the great spirit of the Egyptians, the divine spirit."

The Eternal and Infinite God
"God is the eternal one, he is eternal and infinite; and endures forever and aye; he has endured for countless ages, and he shall endure to all eternity."

The God Of Truth
"God is truth, and he lives truth, and he feeds thereon. He is the king of truth, he rests upon truth, he fashioned truth, and he executes truth throughout all the world."

The God Of Life
"God is life, and through him only man lives. He gives life to man, and he breathes the breath of life into his nostrils."

Again, as stated by learned scholar and Egyptologist E.A. Wallis Budge:

"…these wonderful compositions cover a period of more than five thousand years, and they reflect faithfully….the sublime beliefs, and the high ideals, and noble aspirations of the Egyptians"

Here, I will list one more of the endearing religious texts of the ancient Egyptians:

"God is merciful unto those who reverence him, and he hears him that calls upon him. He protects the weak against the strong, and he hears the cry of him that is bound in fetters; he judges between the mighty and the weak. God knows him that knows him, he rewards him that serves him, and he protects him that follows him."

When this awe-inspiring theology became taught into the learning of the Greek mind, it, of course, poured into the Europe of antiquity. Along with it came the eye witness accounts from those Greek scholars and philosophers, testifying that the priests from whom they had learned these eternal truths were the Black priests of Egypt in Africa.

My personal spiritual quest in-life has not taken me down the paths of exploration into the religious beliefs of such ancient Black civilizations as the Ethiopians or Babylonians or Sumerians etc. However, I feel justified in saying that it is highly unlikely that they did not have a belief system that was in some ways similar to the religious beliefs of the Black civilizations of the ancient Egyptians.

Sir Godfrey Higgins, a well-known orientalist of nineteenth century England produced a literary work in 1836 titled: *Anaclypsis, Or An Inquiry Into The Languages, Nations, and Religions.* In this literary work Sir Godfrey Higgins states the following: "Not only is it true that the people of the Bible were Black….the God Christ, as well as his mother, are described in their old pictures to be Black…the infant God in the arms of his Black mother, his eyes and drapery white, is himself perfectly Black."

By these accounts which we have just read from many witnesses it seems obvious to us that our ancient fathers found God. And it was this amazing *life-changer* of finding God that seems to have become the foundation upon which they formed their faith and built their great civilizations.

If *our* present generation is going-to find God it is only going-to happen in our lifestyle of *worship*. To believe that God really does exist is a wonderful thing. But *finding* God means that we as believers will have added something *more* to our belief that He *exists*. By adding a lifestyle of *worship* to our belief in the existence of God will mean that we shall have decided to *open* ourselves (heart and soul) to the *Spirit* of the living God so that there is no spiritual place within us which is in resistance to God's Spirit becoming revealed *to* us, and becoming present *in* us:

"JESUS SPOKE these things; and lifting up his eyes to heaven, He said, 'Father, the hour has come; glorify Your Son, that the Son may glorify You, even as You gave Him authority over all flesh, that to all whom You have given Him, He may give eternal life. This is eternal life, that they may know You, the only true God, and Jesus Christ whom You have sent.....The glory which You have given Me I have given to them, that they may be one, just as We are one; I in them and You in Me, that they may be perfected in unity, so that the world may know that You sent Me, and loved them, even as You have loved Me'." **John 17:1-3, 22-23** New American Standard Version

If we truly wish to *find* God and if we truly desire to have God *reveal* himself to us, then, the *second* requirement (after *believing* that God exists) is us *loving* God; even though we have not seen him. Our true spiritual *worship* is *us* loving God. It is this true spiritual worship of God that brings-about *Beginnings*. And it is in these *Beginnings* that our *being* becomes *instilled* with Concepts and Perception from God. It is how *vision* becomes manifest into *reality*. Let us begin to pursue a personal revelation with the glorious God of our fathers, the God of our Lord and Savior Jesus Christ.

Part One

HEAVEN'S TREASURE IN EARTHEN VESSELS

*This is the spiritual quest that restores the heart and soul of Black people everywhere.
And fosters peace of heart among all people of every color who will receive it,
in no matter which nation they may be living upon our world.*

MANKIND
OUR WORLD, OUR TIMES, OUR CHOICES

Today in 21st Century civilization a great many of us as Black men and women; and many of our young people as well, struggle with the idea of:

> Who am I as a Black person in today's world?
> Where do I fit-in, in relation to this present civilization which I am living?
> What (if anything) is God looking to do with me here and now?
> When, if *ever* (in my life-time) will I begin to *know* that God's plan is being revealed within me?
> How can I sense if God is reaching-out to me in order to get my attention?
>   (so that: if there *is* some great plan that He has for my life, that plan can become made known to me)

There is a particularly straight-forward and direct passage of scripture in the New Testament, in which God addresses these kind of questions for us, with a great summary concerning MAN and the TIMES. This scripture helps us to focus our thoughts in regards to God's planned AGES for the DESTINIES of various nations of people pertaining to us all as humankind here on Earth: *"The God who made the world and everything in it is the Lord of heaven and earth and does not live in temples built by hands. And he is not served by human hands, as if he needed anything, because he himself gives all men life and breath and every thing else. From one man he made every nation of men, that they should inhabit the whole earth; and he determined the exact times set for them and the exact places where they should live. God did this so that men would seek him and perhaps reach out for him and find him, though he is not far from each one of us. For in him we live and move and have our Being..."*
Acts 17:24-28 New International Version

We; you and I who are this present generation of 21st Century civilization, no matter where we are living in this world, no matter what the circumstances were that has placed us here, God had already known (and planned) that we each would be where we are, before we even arrived here!   That is DESTINY!

Now, in order to become an HEIR of destiny means that right where you are, you must begin to *believe* that God has a *purpose* and a *plan* for having located you there. And especially *now*, in *this* particular time in the History of this world. And when you decide that you are going-to co-operate with God, then is when the amazing *glory* of God becomes poured into you by Him. God pours-out His *glory* from His Kingdom of the Heavens in these TIMES which He has pre-determined will be His TIMES for *you*. That is what we've just read in Acts 17:24-28.

Also, it is of significant importance to note that vs.24 begins: *"The God who made the world and everything in it is the Lord of heaven and earth"*. This word 'Lord' means; of course, that God *rules* over all of His created kingdoms. The Lord God rules over His kingdom of Heaven (or, the Heavens)! And, the Lord God rules over His kingdom of Earth as well. This does not imply that kings and other rulers, governors and leaders of nations who are living upon the earth are ruling in co-operation with God or abiding by God's plan for the Earth. But what this vs.24 does tell us is that no matter if our human leaders will co-operate with God, or not, it is God's rule and authority that will stand. And it is God's *purposes* that will come-to-pass!....both in the Heavens and upon the Earth.

Now, God's rule over His kingdom of the Heavens is very important to us as mankind here on the Earth because it *affects* us here. Let us take, for instance, the TIMES in which Jesus Christ would be born: *"In those days came John the Baptist, preaching in the wilderness of Judaea, And saying, Repent ye: for the kingdom of heaven is at hand."*   **Matthew 3:1-2** King James Version

John the Baptist was telling the people of his generation: *'change your way of thinking, because God's pre-determined Times have come, in which His rule and authority that He has set in the Heavens, will affect our lives here upon the Earth'.*

The phrase *'kingdom of heaven'* (which translates literally to read: *'kingdom of the heavens'*) is a phrase that we find most often repeated in Matthew's gospel about Christ. Nineteenth century theologian and Bible editor C.I. Scofield says (in the Old Scofield Study System *King James Version*) that this phrase *'kingdom of the heavens'* is in reference to 'the rule of the Heavens over the Earth'. Jesus; in Matthew 6:10 (as he prays the Lord's Prayer) gives credence and confirmation to the fact of this *rule of the Heavens over the Earth*. In this one short verse Jesus asks of God the Father that He let *begin* the pre-ordained harmonious union between that which is in the *heavens*, with that which is in the *earth*: *"Thy kingdom come. Thy will be done in earth, as it is in heaven."*

The Lord's Prayer is a prayer for *purging* and *cleansing* the earth. It is a prayer for *re-ordering* the Dispensations and Destinies of *men*, and re-ordering *life* upon the earth. God re-orders these things in accordance with His 'will' for man and the earth. He does this so that the nations and peoples who live upon the earth shall each (in their Times) become *inspired*, *led* and *empowered* to fulfill His purposes and to fulfill His 'will'. No nation or peoples on the earth is excluded from this beneficent 'will' of God. God's gracious and merciful 'will' for the nations and peoples of the earth, is that they each in their predetermined AGE and TIMES shall complete the works of His predestined purposes and plans for them.

It is during the AGE and TIMES of the predetermined *will*, *purposes* and *plans* of God for His people that they can then begin to accomplish upon the earth those things that God has predestined them to accomplish as they co-labor together with Him. Their co-laboring together with God (according to His *will*) also signifies a special spiritual bond of union that they enjoy with *one another*. It is this spiritual bond of union that also harmonizes them together in the certain AGE of God's destiny for them. However, God *first* declares in the *heavens* when it *is* the certain AGE and TIMES of their destiny upon *Earth*. So, in the Lord's Prayer, Jesus Christ is asking of God the Father: *'your kingdom that is now in these specific times declaring your glory in the heavens, let that kingdom also now become established in the earth, and glorify you here as well'*.

The nations of peoples whom the heavens are now declaring that this present moment in history is the Age of your Times, it is *you* who are God's Heirs of Destiny. As God's chosen Heirs of Destiny, no matter who you might be, and no matter how hopeless (or desperate) your present circumstances might seem to be right now, you do not have a calling from God to *self-destruct* through such things as drug abuse or alcoholism. Your dependency upon such things will only weaken you, and hinder your emotional and spiritual resolve, so that it becomes almost impossible for you to *know* and to *recognize* when God is communicating to you. Drugs and alcohol affects your mind and *will* in such ways that it also becomes almost impossible for you to *follow* God.

Neither do you have the time or the right, and certainly not God's approval, to carry-out vengeful and raging pursuits of anger against any other human being. Whether it might be an act which is to the destruction of someone's real or personal property, or, whether it is an act by which bodily harm is done to someone. As Heirs of Destiny there are several very important reasons why God requires such commitment to our emotional wholeness, and to righteous conduct from us. Let us allow the word of God to reveal some of God's reasons to us:

Reason #1
"Blessed be the God and Father of our Lord Jesus Christ, who has blessed us with Every spiritual blessing in the heavenly places in Christ, Just as He chose us in Him Before the foundation of the world, that we would be holy and blameless before Him in love. He predestined us to adoption as sons through Jesus Christ to Himself, according to the kind intention of His will…….For we are His workmanship, created in Christ Jesus for good works, which God prepared beforehand so that we would walk in them." **Ephesians 1:3-5; 2:10** New American Standard Version

Reason #2
"Do you not know that you are a temple of God, and that the Spirit of God dwells in you? If any man destroys the temple of God, God will destroy him; for the temple of God is holy, and that is what you are." **1 Corinthians 3:16-17** New American Standard Version

<u>Reason #3</u>
"Or do you not know that your body is a temple of the Holy Spirit who is in you, whom you have from God, and that you are not your own? For you have been bought with a price, therefore glorify God in your body." **1 Corinthian 6:19-20** New American Standard Version

As HEIRS OF DESTINY we Black men and women cannot afford the mental and emotional baggage that comes from filling our spirit and soul with anger and frustration and resentment. But rather, we should be the conduits that are directing God's power of *love* and *forgiveness* so that spiritual healing can flow throughout our entire world. And by our commitment to such loving purposes of God we will begin receiving His power of emotional healing and restoration: for ourselves, and, for all of mankind. As these spiritual qualities of God then flows through us, we each will be a specific spiritual blessing to every person with whom we come into contact. Those are exactly God's intentions for us. That as HEIRS OF DESTINY we would heal our world, having risen above the hurt of our own wounds, and having become restored from our own sense of brokenness.

If we will just look around ourselves, worldwide, we will see the signs of the eroding of our human civilization. And there is no doubt that we are gradually crumbling to pieces before God! Through-out all the AGES humankind has often had to be chastised, rebuked and corrected by our loving heavenly Father. We have rejected Him, denied Him, and rebelled against His merciful authority so often across the millennia of TIME. If it were not for the patience and long-suffering of God toward us, we *all* as a species would long-ago have become extinct off of the earth. None of us; Black, Brown, Red, Yellow or White have done enough in seeking what it is that is God's true *will* for us *all* collectively as mankind.

And what's more, throughout all the AGES that our collective psyche and genetic make-up can recall: in century after century and dispensation after dispensation, in generation after generation, it does not seem to bother our species that *we* (being created in the *image* and *likeness* of God) *should* have by now become much more highly *spiritually* developed than we are. We should be much more matured and grown-up in how we relate to one another and accept one-another as humankind.

It is within each AGE of TIME that God is conditioning us all: humanity as a whole, for the *greatness* to which He has *before ordained* that we should arrive at as a species. God has a lot to say to us (in the Bible) about the AGES. But we seem to *fast-forward* past this important mind-expanding information God has left to us, and we *move-on* in the scriptures, toward other biblical interests. In our *present* generation most often we move toward such biblical interests as: the gaining of wealth; or, expecting God to beat-down our enemies whether they are real or imagined.

For Black men and women these are special times in which our present generation is living. Right now, in our lifetime, God is transforming this world in which we live. These are the times in which we must now make those choices that keep us true to God's greater purposes for *all* of mankind. And most especially we as AFRICAN AMERICANS must be true to God's greater purposes for our children's children far into the future. It is in this present world environment of change and renewal that we each must begin showing ourselves to be more noble and honorable than we have been in recent generations. We must each choose to be a person of value to God in what He is doing *now*, as He renews our world for the AGES.

In these times of personal renewal and new beginnings you must search your soul, and commit your ways to the things that are of God's good purposes. This will empower you, so that you will be an instrument of Love and Peace in the hand of God. No longer can we afford the high price that our own self-indulgences of the present are demanding of us. And, unless we choose to stop now, our present self-indulgences will continue to demand a high price from our *future* generations as well. We have stunted the spiritual growth of several generations of our children. And largely this is because we have been conditioned to concern ourselves more with frivolous personal pursuits. The things that tend to nurture in us a sense of satisfying self. These selfish vanities in us identify us more with this present *fallen* world, than with the noble and glorious plans and purposes of our *just* and *faithful* God and Father.

Even now these higher purposes of God are already *at-work* in this our present generation. But they only become revealed into the souls of those persons (from every walk of life) who are ready to reflect them into these times of transformation.

In every AGE of man, God transforms and re-creates this world, through Love and Peace. When God brings transformation into this world, it is because He is extending to mankind a gracious, benevolent and merciful opportunity to become welcomed into the KINGDOM OF GOD. God's eternal Kingdom *includes* but also *transcends* this un-regenerated world in which we presently live.

To bring order into His Kingdom, God (through Christ and the Holy Spirit) fills with His presence the heart and soul of everyone who will receive Him. Since God is a Spirit He is no respecter of persons. In other words, God produces His NEW BIRTH in the souls of Black men, White men, Red men, Brown men, Yellow men; all who are willing to become His spiritual sons and daughters. And all of these who are true Christians, are also endowed with the nature of God, and filled with a sense of His holy purposes for the salvation and future benefit of our present world. Here in this fallen world, when all is said and done, it must finally be a personal individual choice (by each one of us) to come into the KINGDOM OF GOD.

These times in which we now live are singularly unique for Black men and women everywhere. This is not a statement of rebellion against any other people. It is not a call to mount some far-flung manmade revolution that further divides us. It is just purely a revelation of the Truth. In these present times upon our world, God is manifesting into the consciousness of Black people everywhere, the means and methods for His perfecting of a glorious transformation in humanity and civilization as we know it on earth. That any of us would resist what God Himself is doing in us right now says much in regards to the worldly nature that seems to have taken the soul of our present generation.

God is preparing all true Christians from every walk of life to be the people of *faith* through which He will plant the seeds of spiritual renewal into the soil of hope in our world. But this will require of humanity (and most especially of the church) that first we navigate the waters of change together, and come upon more peaceful shores. It is Black men and women whom God is *presently* placing at the helm of His great ship of Life. And we all as mankind, together, are to find God's way to renewal while upon this glorious voyage which we are now embarked. Sounds cliché? Well it is not! It is the very essence of Truth. We just have-to *receive* it.

Again, God's higher purposes are Love, Peace and Faith. And those higher purposes are honored by us only as we each are in pursuit of: *becoming the person who fulfills God's expectations of us*. To become that person, we must willingly submit ourselves entirely to God. Do not be the person who has compromised in order to become someone who is considered as *great* among souls that are fallen and empty. At-present, many such souls exist in this morally declined reality. The *lower mentality* can never honor God's *higher purposes*. Such vain things as: greed and the lust to have power over others, de-values the Life itself that is in us. By our greed and vanities devastating wars are fostered. And much destruction is brought upon us *all* here in our world.

Our vain mental pursuits are dead works. They keep us from obtaining the greatest possession of all; the *spiritual awakening* that God has created us one and all to come into and enjoy.

It is unfortunate that we humans continue to fail so often at being our best in God's likeness. And we perpetuate our most profound capacity for moral and spiritual failure at those times that are the most opportune for us to benefit the growth and improvement of our whole world and our entire species. When it comes the time for us to yield to the things that are associated with the plans of God for our spiritual maturing, we humans seem to always use those exact same times to try and destroy everything. And in so doing, we place ourselves in a position to be caught in the endless cycle of having to re-build and start-over. We do this in almost every one of our generations. And sadly we have duped ourselves into allowing these failures to be called progress. God's progress is *spiritual renewal* in Christ:

> "WHAT IS the source of quarrels and conflicts among you? Is not

> *the source your pleasures that wage war in your members? You lust and do not have; so you commit murder. You are envious and cannot obtain; so you fight and quarrel. You do not have because you do not ask. You ask and do not receive, because you ask with wrong motives, so that you may spend it on your pleasures."*
> **James 4:1-3** New American Standard Version

When do we stop? When do we decide to honor LIFE? It is the LIFE of *every* human-being that is important to us *one and all*. God has created something that is priceless within each one of us. LIFE! He has done this so that each person makes his or her own predestined contribution to God's plan that He has ordained for us all as *one* species. It is the LIFE within each of us that is so very priceless.

> *"And he said to his disciples, 'For this reason I say to you, do not worry about your life, as to what you will eat; nor for your body, as to what you will put on. For the **LIFE** is more than food, and the body more than clothing'."* **Luke 12:22-23** New American Standard Version

What we must each now concern ourselves with is such pursuits as will bring our entire family of humanity to discover our true *Being* in God through God's Son, our Lord and Savior Christ Jesus. No person is *born* selfish or evil. It is only as we may yield ourselves to selfish and vain *intentions* that we expose ourselves to becoming influenced (and even guided) by greed and evil.

There is no person living upon our world who is not an HEIR OF DESTINY. The quest that we each must face is: we have each been given choices that affect our own lives and the quality of life for other humans here on earth. So it is important that we all learn to work together in every generation. We must commit ourselves to working together as one family, in the peace of spirit and soul.

God is ever evolving our species toward becoming manifest as higher sentient beings. LIFE is God's vast creation that is to be explored by us, so that we may learn from it. But during every generation of our kind while we are here on earth we seem to be missing the most meaningful lessons that LIFE in *this* world is intended to teach us.

So we should not be surprised that we human beings have difficulty entering those *higher* spiritual realms of God. Realms where we can enjoy the peaceful and awakening benefits that come with experiencing those more pure aspects and realities of the creation life that God has set in order.

Throughout all of LIFE across the vast ocean of God's creation every microbe is in its perfect place. Even in the most threatening asteroid that streaks across the heavens above us, and in the most violent volcano that erupts here upon the earth with us. Every microbe is in its perfect place. Except *within* us!

And there is no doubt that the only reason why God's perfection is not yet manifest *within* us, is because *inside* us (in our fallen state) we resist the perfect *will* and *order* of God, that He has intended for man. God has created man with the freedom and ability to choose. And, we use this great gift of choice, to choose to *resist* our God and Creator.

We resist God's *order* for us as His people. And we resist God's *will* for this world that He has entrusted to our care. We resist God's *glory*, because the things of this *material* world seem to be more important to so many of us. Even more important than the beauty and glory of the *Eternal* that God has created and placed *within* each of us. This same beauty and glory that is *within* us, is from that which God has created and placed in the Heavens also, throughout all the cosmos.

> *"THE HEAVENS declare the glory of God; and the firmament showeth his handiwork."* **Psalm 19:1** King James Version

Our rebellious world must become transformed and brought into the KINGDOM OF GOD. Even though now, of a certainty, this world is one that is *stayed* by the daunting restrictions of these mundane and *temporal* shores. It is here upon these shores of *time* that we labor so feverishly to deprive and subjugate one another. We should rather co-operate with the plans that our loving God has established for effecting *eternity*. It is here upon these temporal shores that we lose sight of the truth concerning: who it really is that God our heavenly Father has *created* us to be:

> *"Beloved, now are we the children of God, and it doth not yet appear what we shall be: but we know that, when he shall appear, we shall be like him; for we shall see him as he is."*
> **1 John 3:2** King James Version

A more celestial existence is most certainly to be desired and welcomed by many of us. But, the love of this labor in the spirit, that we know fulfills the purposes of God in the souls of men here in this our present world, is to be greatly sought after. Because it is by far of a greater benefit and reward for us all right now.

> *"Therefore we are always confident, knowing that, while we are at home in the body, we are absent from the Lord: (For we walk by faith, not by sight:) We are confident, I say, and willing rather to be absent from the body, and to be present with the Lord. Wherefore we labor, that, whether present or absent, we may be accepted of him. For we must all appear before the judgment seat of Christ; that every one may receive the things done in his body, according to that he has done, whether it be good or bad."*
> **2 Corinthians 5:6-10** King James Version

In every generation of mankind we suffer spiritual set-backs, because our personal priorities and agendas here upon the earth are of much greater importance to us than are the higher purposes of God our creator. We are one species, created, all, by the hand of our loving God. We are one family. The differences in the make-up of our *being* as humans are mainly superficial differences, and quite miniscule.

We have all come from one *Father Spirit*. And because of this we should all be enjoying together here on Earth a great and progressive family reunion that produces the higher development of our entire human species. But we miss the point. We *each* lie to *ourselves*, we *all* lie to *God*, and we lie to one another. And we expect <u>freedom</u>, <u>progress</u> and <u>improvement</u> to become produced out of this. They <u>cannot</u>:

> *"Finally, brethren, whatsoever things are true, whatsoever things are honest, whatsoever things are just, whatsoever things are pure,*

whatsoever things are lovely, whatsoever things are of good report;
if there be any virtue, and if there be any praise, think on these things."
Philippians 4:8 King James Version

We the human species should all be engaged harmoniously together in building-up our entire species, one and all. We should be progressively building-up this our world that our Father has entrusted to us. We should be developing advances that reaches and empowers every culture and society across the broad spectrum of our entire human civilization. There should be a greater concern for improvement in such basic and simple areas of our world civilization as housing, producing and distributing food, higher education, technology and communications. Then will God allow us the benefits of a space exploration program that will traverse the heavens and open-up more of His created cosmos to us.

We are God's children and we should be reaching for the stars. But instead we seem to always be caught-up in the childish plots and schemes of the age-old family feud scenario. Our foremost advances as a species should be in the areas that foster peace among governments and nations. We compete against one another far too much. *Co-operation* is always better and far more enriching to our kind than *Competition* is. We forget that we are our Father's children, and so we compete and fight over everything! Shame on us! When do we begin to grow-up?

It is in the harmony of working together, that we engage ourselves in the eternal plans of those endeavors that God Himself is right-now bringing-to-pass for the generations of our children and descendants of the coming *AGE*. Ours is the technological and communications generation to lay those foundations, to the glory of God.

Every people group has been created with something of God *inside* them, which will (in their Time) lead them to build great civilizations that contribute to the on-going harmonious spiritual growth of our species as a whole. But in every generation, it is the greed and the lust for power that is within some of us, that leads them (being the most spiritually weak among us) to look for ways to ensnare others of us. And while this cannot stop the eternal plans of God, it nevertheless is one of the major causes of much human suffering.

In every generation, regardless of what some of us may convince ourselves to believe it is that *we* (in our times) are *achieving*, or, that *we* are *preventing* in our times. It is first foremost and always *God* who is accomplishing *His* holy purposes upon the Earth for the benefit of *all* mankind, by His glorious manifestation of the Children of God into every generation. The only choice that *we* each must now make in *our* generation is: either to *co-operate* with God (or not) in what He is now *bridging* forward to our coming generations of the future in this world AGE which we now stand.

We are God's creation. But a spiritual, mental and emotional *fall* took place from within the high sense of God-consciousness that we had at-first enjoyed. Before the fall we were more sensitive and aware of God's presence in our midst. The fall that took place came as a result of some choices and actions taken by our fore parents Adam and Eve. These choices and actions were born out of Adam and Eve's decisions to *resist* God's authority by disobeying Him. The fall also initiated other effects within our *human* nature. These effects in our nature keeps us human beings further removed from sensing God's presence, and, keeps us continuing to *resist* the plans and authority of God.

But also since the fall, we humans have been redeemed. And, just as at-first we were created in God's own image, we have found that we can now become *re*-created in Jesus Christ our Savior. And once again we can come closer to God.

> *"Therefore, if anyone is in Christ, he is a new creation; the old has gone, the new has come."* **2 Corinthians 5:17** New International Version

God, by His own mercy and grace has done this, so that all who will accept Christ as Savior and Lord will become restored to their exalted position in the Father as Children of God. Today it is these Children of God now living in this our present generation and being called-forth by God from *every walk of life*, it is *they* who are the HEIRS OF DESTINY.

They must each begin to nurture a genuine desire for becoming a part of God's plan for them. They will be instrumental to God in His plan to awaken us all.

And, they will usher-in some amazing transformations upon our world, because it is God who is using them in manifesting what He is doing.

As we enter this first day of the risen AGE, we must walk in the assurance that the TIMES of God's Spirit of Destiny *lives now* within the grasp of our present generation. And, in faith, we must set ourselves to the task of pursuing the holy *purposes* of God. Such holy purposes as God himself will most certainly reveal into our spirit and soul.

Every human soul upon the earth is important to God. And every one of us has a predestined role to play in what God is doing now.

We are each a free moral agent. God has created us with this gifted ability to freely choose that we will either be committed to what He is doing, or, to follow our own plans that we establish for ourselves. It is our choices and motives that will determine the position we will each take in what this AGE of God will produce in Man under the Heavens. I do not know who will choose what. And neither do you. But I *do* know that we will recognize those who will have chosen to be God's Heirs in all of this. Because, whoever they are, it is the Love of God, the Peace of God, and, their Faith in God that will be evident in their nature, their character and their personality. They will want to serve the purposes of God.

Searching My Heart

ABOUT

_____

MANKIND
OUR WORLD, OUR TIMES, OUR CHOICES

1. In further developing all of humanity into a higher state of spiritual being: Love, Peace and Faith are three of the most important things to God.
   What does that mean to me? Here's what I believe it means to be a person of Love, Peace and Faith.

   _____
   _____
   _____

2. What are some things that I can begin to do in order to better help me connect with God's purposes for me in these present TIMES?

   _____
   _____
   _____

3. What are some things that I can begin to do in order to better help me connect with other human beings who may be searching for the truths of God as I am?

   _____
   _____
   _____

4. Do I believe God has a higher purpose for my life by me working together with others in Love, Peace and Faith? If *Yes,* why? If *No,* why not?

   _____
   _____
   _____

AFRICA
CREATION, CIVILIZATION and a FADING ILLUMINATION

Africa is the continent upon which God created man. Today scientists of many different disciplines such as *archaeology, human genetics,* and *anthropology,* are more and more inclined to agree that the continent of Africa is the place where human life began on planet Earth.

This is largely due to the increase of information from scientific explorations that continue to yield interesting facts supporting the African origins of creation. It is also a commonly known and accepted fact today, that it was in the far distant ancient past that the earliest civilizations of man were first established. And those too, were on the continent of Africa. Those earliest ancient civilizations were established by Africans. Africa is the homeland and origins of the Black peoples and nations.

Over the centuries and across the millennia we the peoples of Africa seem to have lost something that is a wonderful Divine Spark which is inside us. And, as a consequence, we became lost. It was as if the fire inside us was dying.

But the fire did *not* die! It was just that we had become so attentive to our own wants. Our focus became more toward what *we* wanted, rather than to what *God* wanted *for* us. It was this vain sense of our self-entitlement, which marked the beginning of our long decline. The developing of our civilizations; our way, became more important to us than anything else. And so, we no longer looked to the fire inside us. We had stopped looking for that fire to guide us. With its divine light of illumination in the deepest most spiritual reaches of our *Being*. We had surely lost our bearing, and we had lost our way. Becoming *lost* changes everything. It changes how you think, how you feel, how you respond to different circumstances. It changes everything.

What It Can Mean To Be *Lost*:

1) To not know *Where* you are:
    Lost from knowing the *Location* that God has allotted on Earth as His place for you to live

"And hath made of one blood all nations of men for to dwell on all the face of the earth, and hath determined the times before appointed, and <u>the bounds of their habitation</u>."
                                                  Acts 17:26 King James Version

2) To not know *Who* you are:
    Lost from knowing the spiritual *Heritage* that God fore-ordained for you

"Come, ye blessed of my Father, <u>inherit the kingdom</u> prepared for you from the foundation of the world."
                                Matthew 25:34 King James Version

3) To not know *Why* you are:
    Lost from knowing God's predestined *Purpose* for your life

"I press toward the mark for the prize of the <u>high calling of God</u> in Christ Jesus. Let us therefore, as many as be perfect, be thus minded: and if in any thing ye be otherwise minded, <u>God shall reveal even this unto you</u>."   **Philippians 3:14-15** King James Version

4) To not know *When* you are:
    Lost from knowing God's plans for you right *Now* in this present generation and time

"But <u>ye are a chosen generation</u>, a royal priesthood, an holy nation, a peculiar people; that ye should show forth the praises of him who hath <u>called you out of darkness</u> into his marvelous light."
                              1 Peter 2:9 King James Version

5) To not know *What* you are:
    Lost from being aware of how *Precious* and *Valuable* you are to God

"And when he [Jesus] was come near, he beheld the city, and <u>wept over it</u>, Saying, If thou hadst known, even thou, at least <u>in this thy day</u>, the <u>things which belong unto thy peace</u>! But now they are hid from thine eyes." **Luke 19:41-42** King James Version [brackets mine]

In God's great plans and purposes for the AGES, nations and tribes and peoples and tongues rise and fall. In bringing fallen man to restoration, God allows us all to have our TIMES of founding, developing and growing our great civilizations. All nations of people; once they reach a certain level in their social, cultural and civic development come to the Times (in their civilization) when they feel that they no-longer need God to guide them. They've become technologically advanced, very productive self-sufficient and all-wise. Or, so they convince themselves to believe.

It is difficult to say whether it is their technological advances, or, organized religion or political influence, military might or any combination of things that has brought them to feel superior. But it happens to every nation of people whom God has graciously allowed to prosper and enjoy periods of affluence in this world. They convince themselves to believe that it is they themselves who has brought this progress unto themselves. We must all allow God's warnings to Israel (as they were nearing the time of entering their promised land) be also His warnings to us:

> *"When the LORD your God brings you into the land he swore to your fathers, to Abraham, Isaac, and Jacob, to give you --- a land with large, flourishing cities you did not build, houses filled with all kinds of good things you did not provide, wells you did not dig, and vineyards and olive groves you did not plant --- then when you eat and are satisfied, be careful that you do not forget the LORD, who brought you out of Egypt, out of the land of slavery. Fear the LORD your God, serve him only and take your oaths in his name."*
>
> **Deuteronomy 6:10-13** New International Version

This our present 21st Century generation has finally come. It is in these our days, that we can now look to God our heavenly Father to rekindle the smoldering embers of our spiritual fire. This *fire* of the Spirit of God is Heaven's Treasure in these earthen vessels which we live. The treasure *within* is God's priceless gift to us, so that we can receive His *divine guidance*. However, in order to rekindle this *fire*, we will first need to re-discover the ancient biblical seed from which our present African lineages are descended. The Bible records much information about our ancestral fathers. It is information about those who trusted God long before the *coming-to-be* of this our present generation. And we can be proud to be their descendants.

> *"LORD THOU hast been our dwelling-place in all generations. Before the mountains were brought forth, or even thou had formed the earth or the world, even from everlasting to everlasting, thou art God. Thou turns man to destruction; and say, Return, ye children of men. For a thousand years in thy sight are but as yesterday when it is past, and as a watch in the night."* **Psalm 90:1-3** King James Version

Our goal in HEIRS OF DESTINY is to bring us as Africans back to a secure and trusting *faith* in God. It is our faith in God as human-beings which will lead us all into the personal assurance that God's Divine Spark *still lives* inside each one of us today.

And God's Divine Spark living within each one of us, is for His *purposes* and *glory*. It is also this same *faith* of which we've mentioned, that first will *re-awaken* us, in *this our present* generation. We will come to the realization of that which God now desires, which is: to restore *all* humanity to the sense of *Heaven's Treasure* (that we each possess) in these *Earthen Vessels* which we now live.

In our present generation, as Black men and women, God will use our restored *faith-life* in His plan for blessing all of mankind.

We will concern ourselves here with reclaiming our sense of human self-worth. But more than that, our entire family of humanity shall also reclaim here our Godly dignity and our spiritual fortitude.   We will raise the consciousness of Black people in particular, by using the Bible.   And by the stirring accounts of some of the remarkable achievements of our ancient African fathers. These are the things which led to the founding of the many great civilizations that they built.

> *"For God, who commanded the light to shine out of darkness, hath shined in our hearts, to give the light of the knowledge of the glory of God in the face of Jesus Christ. But we have this treasure in earthen vessels, that the excellency of the power may be of God, and not of us.* **2 Corinthians 4:6** KJV

AFRICA
THE LAND OF HAM

*ANTEDILUVIAN CIVILIZATION
*[civilization *before* the Flood]*

Read Genesis 6:1 – 9:19

GOD ESTABLISHES HIS COVENANT OF BLESSING

<u>THE NOAHIC COVENANT</u>   review *Genesis 9:1-19*

1. In *Genesis 9:1* who does the scripture say is included in the **Blessing** from God?

_____
write your answer here

2. In *Genesis 9:8-9* who does the scriptures say God established his **Covenant** with ?

_____
write your answer here

Modern sciences that provide research and study results from such disciplines as *genetic anthropology,* and the *ancient migrations [ie exoduses]* of people groups, have determined that all human people groups today had as their place of origin the continent of Africa. This means that all humans are of one common African bloodline. Our mixed lineages and colors result from the early AGES of migrations/exoduses, and from generations of mixed-breeding within our human species.

"And *[God] hath made of <u>one blood</u> all nations of men to dwell on all the face of the earth….."   **[brackets mine]*
Acts 17:26 King James Version

NOAH
[and his sons]

SHEM   HAM   JAPHETH

THE TABLE OF NATIONS   review *Genesis 10:1-32*

1. In *Genesis 10:6* the scripture lists the four sons of Ham. These are **Noah's grandsons**. And they are important to us.

   Write down the names of the sons of Ham:

   _____ , _____ , _____ , _____

2. In *Genesis 10:7-20* read the brief account concerning some of the *grandsons* of Ham. Think on the great things the scriptures say they accomplished, and the vast expanses of their civilizations. These are **Noah's great-grandsons**. And they are important to us.

3. Why are Noah's **grandsons**, and **great-grandsons** (under Ham) so important to us? They are, because it means that we as the descendant Black nations of Africa are included in the COVENANT that GOD has established with Noah and with Ham! The NOAHIC COVENANT includes **us**:

   *"And you, be ye fruitful, and multiply, bring forth abundantly in the earth, and multiply therein. And God spake unto **Noah**, and to his **sons** with him, saying, And I, behold, I establish my covenant with you, and with your **seed** after you"*   Genesis 9:7-9   King James Version

   When God said to Noah and to his son Ham: *"your **seed** after you"*, that refers to you and me, **us**! We are included in the Covenant that God made with Noah.

Now, as Black people, we can all agree that this is very good information for us to have. Nevertheless, the Bible warns us of becoming caught-up in the melodramatic attraction of such subjects as blood-lineages and genealogies.

> *"Neither give heed to fables and endless genealogies, which minister questions, rather than godly edifying which is in faith: so do."* **1 Timothy 1:4** King James Version

However, having said that, we can also find great comfort in the fact that God has a purpose and plan for having placed in His Holy Word this information about our ancient heritage to Noah (through Ham). God has done this so that in our present 21st Century generation, we as the *dispersed seed* *[Dia*spora*] can have a living hope; and a sense of patriarchal pride in our ancestral lineages.

We have come now into these *times* in which God has predestined that we, as Africans, are to do amazing things by His guiding hand, and for His glorious purposes. I do not know who my paternal and maternal grandparents *were* from six or eight or ten generations into the *past*. More especially I do not know them from as far back as three or four or five thousand years ago. Neither do you know who your long-ago ancient forefathers were.

But we *do* know that they were African. And, we *do* know that they lived and loved and discovered and built, and ruled and invented and governed, and died. And, they did *much* of these things on a *grand* scale. Then, having *passed into the heavens*, they entered the *higher* realms of God's glory. And for this information having been left to us through the Holy Bible I am truly *thankful* to God, because it fills me with a sense of encouragement, purpose, hope and expectation.

> *"Wherefore seeing we also are compassed about with so great a cloud of witnesses, let us lay aside every weight, and the sin which doth so easily beset us, and let us run with patience the race that is set before us. Looking unto Jesus the author and finisher of our faith..."*
> **Hebrews 12:1-2a** King James Version

GOD'S BIBLICAL ACCOUNT of OUR ANCIENT AFRICAN FATHERS UNDER NOAH and HAM

NOAH

HAM

HAMITES [The sons of Ham - *Genesis 10:6-8*]

CUSH	MIZ'RA'IM	PUT/PHUT	CA'NAAN		
[Ethiopia]	[Egypt – *Gen. 10:13-14*]	[Lybia]	[Canaanites – *Gen. 10:15-18*]		
Seba	Ludim		Sidon/Zidon [once Capital of ancient Phoenicia]		
Havilah	Anamim		Heth [Hittites]	Hivites	Arvadites
Sabtah	Lehabim		Jebus [Jebusites]	Arkites	Zemarites
Raamah [Sheba Gen. 10:7]	Naphtuhim		Amorites	Sinites	Hamathites
Sabteca	Pathrusim		Girgashites		
*Nimrod [Gen. 10:8-12; see 'Babel'; Isaiah 13:1 and Rev. 18:2 notes]	Casluhim [father of the Phillistines] Caphtorim				

About You As a Black Person, and The Sons of Ham

From ADAM to NOAH and HAM...

> "*Adam, Seth, Enosh, Kenan, Mahalaleel, Jared, Enoch, Methuselah, Lamech, Noah, Shem, Ham, and Japheth.*"
> **1 Chronicles 1:1-4** King James Version

> "*The sons of HAM: Cush, and Mizraim, Put, and Canaan. And the sons of Cush: Seba, and Havilah, and Sabta, and Raama, and Sabteca. And the sons of Raama: Sheba, and Dedan. And Cush begot Nimrod; he began to be mighty upon the earth. And Miz'raim begot Ludim, and An'amim, and Lehabim, and Naphtuhim, And Pathrusim, and Casluhim (of whom came the Phillistines), and Caphtorim. And Canaan begot Sidon, his first-born, and Heth, The Jebusite also, and the Amorite, and the Girgashite, And the Hivite, and the Arkite, and the Sinite, And the Arvadite, and the Zemarite, and the Hamathite.*"
> **1 Chronicles 1:8-16** King James Version

- **CUSH / ETHIOPIA** [son of Ham, son of Noah]   Read *Gen. 10:7*

    SHEBA [a son of ETHIOPIA]

The Queen of SHEBA

The Bible doesn't say very much about the man named SHEBA who was the son of ETHIOPIA. However, we do know historically (concerning the land) that his tribal groups of ancient Africa were not much different than some African tribes even in more recent history, in that they had their tribal lands and territories.

We read also in the scriptures, that a certain *queen* of one of the ancient Ethiopian tribal lands of Sheba came to visit King Solomon:

> *"And when the queen of Sheba heard of the fame of Solomon concerning the name of the LORD, she came to [prove] him with hard questions. And she came to Jerusalem with a very great train, with camels that bore spices, and very much gold, and precious stones; and when she was come to Solomon, she [talked] with him of all that was in her heart. And Solomon [answered] all her questions; there was not any thing hid from the king, which he told her not."*
> **1 Kings 10:1-3** King James Version

It appears here, according to the scriptures, that this Ethiopian *queen* from the land of Sheba was interested in meeting Solomon because of his noble reputation *"concerning the name of the LORD"*. In the Old Testament the word written as *'LORD'* was in direct reference to GOD almighty. And according to the scriptures the queen of Sheba journeyed to meet with Solomon so that she could ask him what the Bible text refers to as the *"hard questions"*.

The text says the queen of Sheba did this so that she could *"prove"* Solomon. As if to ask of Solomon: do you *really know* of the LORD [GOD almighty]?
According to the customs of those days, the queen of Sheba brought with her (as gifts to the king) spices and gold and precious stones from her own land.

Based upon the way the writing of 1 Kings 10:1 flows: *"And when the queen of Sheba heard of the fame of Solomon concerning the name of the LORD, she came to prove him with hard questions"*, it is not unthinkable for a reasonable mind to believe it likely that this queen of Sheba herself perhaps *already knew* of the LORD [GOD almighty]. It seems as if the queen of Sheba wanted to assure herself that Solomon's noble reputation concerning the LORD [GOD almighty] was indeed true.

Apparently, by the time this queen of Sheba was ready to return to her own land she had satisfied her concerns about Solomon's knowledge of the LORD [GOD almighty]. Also, it is quite obvious that she herself had made a considerable personal impression upon king Solomon based upon the manner in which he responds to her visit:

> *"And King Solomon gave unto the queen of Sheba all her desire, whatsoever she asked, beside that which Solomon gave her of his royal bounty. So she turned and went to her own country, she and her servants."* **1 Kings 10:13** King James Version

It seems here that there was nothing in the land that the queen of Sheba could ask from Solomon: *"all her desire, whatsoever she asked"* that he did not give to her. Even out of those things which were Solomon's *"royal bounty"*, or, riches from within his own personal treasury as king.

NIMROD [a son of ETHIOPIA]

<u>The Mighty Hunter-King</u>

It is an unquestionable truth that the Black people have a profound ability to lead, build, govern, invent, manifest the fruit of an amazing creative artistry; and so very much more. But what did we lose from within ourselves that we seem to be having such a difficult time regaining?

> *"And Cush begat Nimrod: he began to be a mighty one in the earth. He was a mighty hunter before the LORD: wherefore it is said, Even as Nimrod the mighty hunter before the LORD. And the beginning of his kingdom was Babel, and Erech, and Accad, and Calneh, in the land of Shinar. Out of that land went forth Asshur, and builded Nineveh, and the city Rehoboth, and Calah, And Resen between Nineveh and Calah: the same is a great city."*
> **Genesis 10:8-12** King James Version

Our ancient forefather NIMROD founded a kingdom which was so vast and far-reaching in its expanse until it seems to be an almost unimaginable task for us to try and scale it to our capacity for perception. The Bible just describes Nimrod's kingdom in this way: *"And the **beginning** of his kingdom was Babel, and Erech, and Accad, and Calneh, in the land of Shinar."* **Genesis 10:10**

It is obvious in the text for us to notice that under Nimrod's leadership there were *other* leaders who *also* became equipped for greatness: *"Out of that land went forth Asshur, and builded Nineveh, and the city Rehoboth, and Calah, And Resen between Nineveh and Calah: the same is a great city."* **Genesis 10:11-12**

But something happened with our ancestors in the land of Shinar. Something changed within them. The Bible is not clear as to whether this change took-place during the days of Nimrod's leadership, or if it was after. And frankly it doesn't matter whether it was during or after the days of Nimrod. The change did take-place within us. The change was not in a good way. And it happened in Shinar, which was where Nimrod's far-reaching kingdom had its beginning:

"And the whole earth was of one language, and of one speech. And it came to pass, as they journeyed from the east, that they found a plain in the land of Shinar; and they dwelt there. And they said one to another, Go to, let us make brick, and burn them throughly. And they had brick for stone, and slime had they for mortar. And they said, Go to, let us build us a city with a tower, whose top may reach unto heaven; and let us make us a name, lest we be scattered abroad upon the face of the whole earth. And the LORD came down to see the city and the tower, which the children of men builded. And the LORD said, Behold, the people is one, and they have all one language; and this they begin to do: and now nothing will be restrained from them, which they have imagined to do. Go to, let us go down, and there confound their language, that they may not understand one another's speech. So the LORD scattered them abroad from thence upon the face of all the earth..." **Genesis 11:1-8** King James Version

This was at Shinar, where the *'beginning'* of Nimrod's kingdom had been, in Africa, the land of Noah and his son Ham; the land of the Black peoples.

This is not about Black is better than White, or Brown is better than Yellow. This is about a *people* who need to regain their sense of hope, dignity and Godly *Being*. It is about a people beginning to see themselves again as God's great people.

Ambition is the cunning enemy *within* us that wars *against* us in the fulfilling of our *Divine Destiny*. It was because of their personal (and corporate) *ambition* that our ancient fathers *lost* something in Shinar at the tower of Babel. That day, they did not *die* on the inside. They just lost their sense of *spiritual certainty* that every *Heir* of God carries within. And so, the *times* which had been the AGE of our ancestors' ever-moving *forward* progress, began to become the times when *"the LORD scattered them abroad."* **Genesis 11:8**

In the spiritual, mental and emotional development of mankind, every nation of people comes to such times as our ancestors of Africa did when they attempted to build the tower of Babel. There is no nation of people (past or present) who are exempt from this vain and self-serving condition that is within our fallen nature as mankind. As our civilizations grow, this self-serving condition within us usually manifests itself in several different ways. One very apparent way is this: as our civilizations develop and flourish, we become arrogant, and we begin to struggle with the notion of thinking ourselves to be all-knowing, all-wise, or even better than someone else.

Whenever we decide to really *take to heart* the lessons that God (by His grace) is teaching us about ourselves. Glorious things will begin to happen in us and among us. The lessons of God's grace are lessons about Love, Peace and Faith. Those are the riches of spirit that brings us to the place of *oneness* with God and with each other. And, it is time for us to decide that we really want the lessons of God to work *in* us! And ***through*** us, ***for*** us! It is only when we ***apply*** these lessons of grace here in our world that we all (as a species) will move-on, together, into greater things. God's progressive plan for the spiritual recovery and development of our entire human potential is a plan that will open to us the fullness of His created universal and cosmic Kingdom:

> *"To me, the very least of all saints, this grace was given, to preach to the Gentiles the unfathomable riches of Christ,"* **Ephesians 3:8** New American Standard Version

Let's Discuss The Bible Verse We've Just Read

The apostle Paul; in writing to the church at Ephesus concerning the truths of God, establishes several remarkable foundations here for *all of mankind* in how we should be relating to God and to one another while we are here in this world:

Point #1   In **verse :8** Paul reminds us that his assignment from God is: *"to preach to the Gentiles the unfathomable riches of Christ."*

> For something to be *unfathomable* simply means that it can be vast and far-reaching in its depth or scope. *Unfathomable* can also mean that something is not necessarily even susceptible to human scrutiny or understanding. Paul also says here that God *gave* him this assignment as an act of God's own *grace*. In other words, Paul had not personally done something that was so remarkably wonderful before God wherein it *entitled* him to this gracious assignment from a loving and benevolent God. And neither have we. But the plans of God are sure.

Point #2   In **verse :8** Paul also mentions the word *Gentiles*:

> According to man's typical understanding of the word *Gentiles* in the Bible, it is a word that is descriptive of all peoples who are not Jews. However, this description would be inconsistent with God's Plans for *all* MANKIND as He, throughout the AGES, moves our *entire species* into a continuing progressive spiritual maturity. It is not in any way here our intention to imply any negative thing about Jews or *any* people. It is just a statement of fact, that the word *Gentile* is a word that is to be associated with *any* people who are *not* God's *Covenant* people at a particular and given *Time* in His *plan* for our species as a whole. And, the word that *is*

associated with the *Covenant* people who *are* God's chosen and elect for a particular given Time, is: ISRAEL.

Israel is a word that means: *'to rule as God'*, or more fittingly *'to rule with God'*. Israel is not a word that is intended to be a definitive word designating *forever* one particular ethnic *group* of people. This means, then, that *whomever* the people may be that God is pouring *His Spirit* and special *plans*, *calling*, *revelations* and *abilities* into during a particular AGE with its many DISPENSATIONS, *They* are the chosen people, God's people of the covenant. It does not really matter what particular walk of life (what ethnicity) they may come from. God's one requirement of them, in order that they become Israel, is that *each one* of them must first accept Christ by *Faith*. Then they are His Covenant people. Then they are ISRAEL.

It would benefit all of mankind, for us all to be reminded, that Israel is *whomever* the people are that God is working *in* and *through* during any given AGE and DISPENSATION. Jesus Christ did that for us *all*!

> *"But the scripture declares that the whole world is a prisoner of sin, so that what was promised, being given through faith in Jesus Christ, might be given to those who believe. Before this faith came, we were held prisoners by the law, locked up until faith should be revealed. So the law was put in charge to lead us to Christ that we might be justified by faith. Now that faith has come, we are no longer under the supervision of the law. You are all sons of God through faith in Christ Jesus, for all of you who were baptized into Christ have clothed yourselves with Christ. There is neither Jew nor Greek, slave nor free, male nor female, for you are all one in Christ Jesus. If you belong to Christ, then are you Abraham's seed, and heirs according to the promise."* **Galatians 3:22-29** New International Version

As *"heirs according to the promise"*, we who are Black peoples need to be seriously contemplating our salvation in Christ. And we need also to be seriously considering who it is that *we are* in the plans of God for these present times which we now live.

In other words, as God has predetermined (and set in order) a specific *Destiny* for you, He can choose to *reveal* it to *you* alone, concealing it from everyone else. Or, God *may* choose to reveal such *portions* as may be necessary, to those who will be *instrumental* to God in some way, in His *plan* to fulfill His holy *purposes* through you. The choice is up to God. And *our* quest, each of us, is to find out from Him, what is His higher meaning and specific purpose for us each as an individual, and collectively as a people. That is what Jesus Christ accomplished for us at the cross. He accomplished it for *all* of mankind.

If you think that Christ accomplished these works of salvation for Black people alone you are mistaken. It is not about what we refer-to as racism, nor is it about you and I being better than someone else. It is about the plans and purposes of God for our *entire species* of Mankind here on Earth. And in every AGE; and certain DISPENSATIONS, God *spiritually* empowers specific *people groups* in order that they may achieve certain and specific accomplishments for the benefit of the entire species of humanity. In these *particular Times* which have just come upon us, it is the Black people whom God is transforming, in order that they become used by Him in special ways.

Now, as HEIRS OF DESTINY all of mankind has the presence of a great *spiritual certainty* within each of us. This spiritual certainty present within us is the vital link that contributes to the continuous maturing of our very *Being* in God. This spiritual certainty is better known as *FAITH*. *Assurance* is---the <u>*awareness*</u> of Faith.

Faith gives to us a sense of confidence. But the other remarkable *in-working* of Faith, is that *with* it comes also the great assurance that it is *God Himself* who is actively *doing* that which is necessary in order to fulfill every *promise* in the *covenant* that He *establishes* with us:

> *"Now faith is the substance of things hoped for, the evidence of things not seen. ...Through faith we understand that the worlds were framed by the word of God, so that things which are seen were not made of things which do appear....By faith Noah, being warned of God of things not seen as yet, moved with fear, prepared an ark to the saving of his house; by the which he condemned the world, and became heir of the righteousness which is by faith."*
> **Hebrews 11:1, 3, 7** King James Version

We Black people are now the *Heirs* of a great *Destiny*. However, *our present generation* has a responsibility to God that we each make the choice to *inherit* the *righteousness* of God (as Noah did) which is ours by *faith*. And also, we have a responsibility to *one another*, to *the world*, and to this AGE that is *upon* us.

Our responsibility as Black people is: to receive from God the power and authority that He is now *pouring out* to us for making this (His entire created world) a better place for *all* of mankind. It will not be easy on our part. It will require a great faith and perseverance from us. But it will not *fail*, because God has already predestinated the next generations of us in order for it to succeed. *"...Our father which art in heaven, Hallowed be thy name. Thy kingdom come. Thy will be done in earth, as it is in heaven. Give us this day our daily bread. And forgive us our debts, as we forgive our debtors. And lead us not into temptation, but deliver us from evil: For thine is the kingdom, and the power, and the glory, for ever. Amen"*   **Matthew 6:9-13** King James Version

- <u>**MIZRAIM /EGYPT**</u> [son of Ham, son of Noah] Read *Gen. 10:6*

<u>The Monuments and Works In Stone Of The ANCIENT EGYPTIANS</u>

Three Pyramids stand upon the Giza Plateau in Egypt. They are the most notable remains that are left to us from the times of a remarkable past. These Pyramids are a kind of mirror in stone that is left for our generations today. They reflect the regal splendor that continues to be the legacy of our great Black fathers and mothers. They are a snapshot of the African civilization that built them, in those far distant ancient days.

Stone! Our ancestors used stone to build the Pyramids. They used stone to build many of their temples of worship. They used stone as tablets upon which they wrote with *ink *(produced from fruit etc) concerning their beliefs in God, and about their ancient world. Over time archaeology and other sciences have offered-up differing opinions as to *when* the Pyramids were actually built.

The most commonly set-forth time(s) for the Pyramids of Giza to have been built fluctuate between 2672 B.C. and 2450 B.C. However, there are also such far distant ancient times as 10500 B.C. that have been set-forth as the times of the building of the Pyramids. So man is unclear as to the date(s) which we could consider as being correct for the building of the Pyramids.

I am a Born-Again Bible believing Christian. The year 2014 will mark 30 years in which I have been truly blessed to continue serving as a pastor before God our heavenly Father, and, before my Savior and Lord Jesus Christ. As I read and study my Bible I do not see anything in the Old (or New) Testament that I believe to be a mention of these amazing stone structures that are the Pyramids.

Yet, that does not dissuade me from being absolutely certain that God has allowed these great monuments and tablets in *stone* to remain here among us; as a constant reminder to us who *are* the Black people, of what we are capable (in Christ) of going beyond achieving even *Today*.

I am not discouraged by the fact that I do not find in my Bible any specific reference to the many great *stone* monuments and tablets left here by the ancient civilizations of our Black fathers. The message that those works in stone were intended to leave for us has over the millennia of time been defaced, damaged, and their meaning detracted from.

But that is alright. God knew those things would happen. In fact, I am even *more* inspired at how God chooses *now* to summon His holy *purposes* into our *heart*; and into our very *spirit* and *soul*, as opposed to the obscure messages of bygone times, that were built up in those works of *dead stones* left stacked upon each other for us by our forefathers. Since Christ has come into our world, we can *now* all find purpose in these *life-giving* words that God has left with us through the apostles Peter and Paul, so that we might *instill* these precious words to our heart:

> *"You also, as living stones, are being built up as a spiritual house for a holy priesthood, to offer up spiritual sacrifices acceptable to God through Jesus Christ. For this is contained in scripture:* BEHOLD, I LAY IN ZION A CHOICE STONE, A PRECIOUS CORNER *stone,* AND HE WHO BELIEVES IN HIM WILL NOT BE DISAPPOINTED.*"*   **1Peter 2:5-6**   New American Standard Version

> *"Forasmuch as ye are manifestly declared to be the epistle of Christ ministered by us, written not with ink, but with the Spirit of the living God; not in tablets of stone, but in the fleshy tablets of the heart. And such trust have we through Christ to Godward: Not that we are sufficient of ourselves to think any thing as of ourselves; but our sufficiency is of God; Who also has made us able ministers of the new testament; not of the letter, but of the spirit: for the letter kills, but the spirit gives life."*   **2 Corinthians 3:3-6**   King James Version

> *"For this is the covenant that I will make with the house of Israel after those days, saith the Lord; I will put my laws into their mind, and write them in their hearts: and I will be to them a God, and they shall be to me a people:"*   **Hebrews 8:10**   King James Version

According to the scriptures we've just read, I do not know of a better or more perfect way to describe for us as Black people, what it is that God himself is doing *in* us today. Now is the time that we each have some personal decisions to make, as to, whether we will receive CHRIST and follow HIM into God's DESTINY for us each. Will we each (by Faith) choose LIFE in Christ? Or will we reject the amazing offer of DESTINY that God is extending to us? Let us not continue to *deny* ourselves this spiritual inheritance of becoming the sons and daughters of God.

There is no science or invention of man that can hide your *future* from you. No matter what effect drugs or alcohol may have upon your *mind*, no matter what mistakes or poor choices you have made in your past, it is not the end for you. The moment you make the decision that you will *trust* God with the plans He has made for your life, things will begin to *change* for you. The moment you surrender your *heart* to God (in Faith) He will begin to prepare you to become led and guided by His Holy Spirit. It doesn't even matter what your particular circumstances *right now* might be, God is *calling* to you. However, becoming *chosen* is up to you.

> *"For by grace you have been saved through faith; and that not of yourselves, it is the gift of God; Not as a result of works, so that no one may boast. For we are His workmanship, created in Christ Jesus for good works, which God prepared beforehand so that we would walk in them."* **Ephesians 2:8-10** New American Standard Version

Your *future* is not in the carved stone-tablets of the *past*. Your *future* is in your *heart* and *soul*. It is in your very *spirit*. You are a *living stone* of the most high and merciful God! You are an HEIR OF DESTINY! BELIEVE it! OWN It! LIVE it!

> *"But we have this treasure in earthen vessels, that the excellency of the power may be of God, and not of us."*
> **2 Corinthians 4:7** King James Version

Israel was in captive bondage in Egypt for over 400 years. The issue of controversy concerning whether the nation of Israel were of Black African descent is not at question here. There is a much more important point here that must be taken to heart. They had been in slavery for more than four centuries. Then, by the hand of God (through Moses) they were delivered and became free.

"And Pharaoh rose up in the night, he, and all his servants, and all the Egyptians; and there was a great cry in Egypt; for there was not a House where there was not one dead. And he called for Moses and Aaron by night, and said, rise up, and get you forth from among my people, both ye and the children of Israel; and go, serve the LORD, as ye have said."
Exodus 12:30-31 King James Version

After Israel had become free, what the many generations of slavery and poverty had produced in their children soon became apparent. Such characteristics as anger and resentment, and doubts fears and phobias of all sorts surfaced from within the psyche of this first free generation who were the descendants of slaves. And most especially, they harbored serious feelings of uncertainty within themselves, as to whether they could succeed on their own, apart from having the help and support they had been accustomed to from the hand-me-down lifestyle of slavery in Egypt.

> *"And they said unto Moses, Because there were no graves in Egypt, hast thou taken us away to die in the wilderness? wherefore hast thou dealt thus with us, to carry us forth out of Egypt? Is not this the word that we did tell thee in Egypt, saying, Let us alone, that we may serve the Egyptians? For it had been better for us to serve the Egyptians, than that we should die in the wilderness."*
> **Exodus 14:11-12** King James Version

God had used *Moses* as their deliverer. To shepherd them *out* from bondage. But before they could *come into* the *Promised Land* that God would use *Joshua* to bring them into, they would first have-to become purged of their resentment, anger, doubts, fears and uncertainty. They would have-to begin to *trust* God.

> *"And Joshua said unto the people, Sanctify yourselves: For tomorrow the LORD will do wonders among you."*
> **Joshua 3:5** King James Version

THE CHANGE THAT OUR CHOICES MAKE

Every choice that I have ever made in my life changed something about my life. And my choices changed something about the lives of people around me as well. This is true not just with my life only, but these same dynamics apply to every person that you and I know. MY personal choices affect ME and many other persons whom I may love or care about. And, so also does YOURS.

Because you are *spirit* living in a *body* God has given to you the ability to bring change! The change that you choose to bring must be change that honors and glorifies God, and manifests His purposes in the lives of others around you. You are either part of God's great *plan* for the *future* of Mankind, or, you're part of the *problem* that brings hurt, pain, and suffering into the lives of so many other people.

List some choices that you wish you had NOT made in your life, and how those choices affected other persons:

1. Choice: _____

    Affect on others: _____

2. Choice: _____

    Affect on others: _____

List some choices you've made that you would like to CHANGE, and how you believe these Choice-Changes will affect other persons:

1. Choice-Change: _____

    How this will affect others: _____

2. Choice-Change: _____

    How this will affect others: _____

Your *destiny* does not lay in the plans of what you or some other human has determined for you. Your *fate* does, based upon the *choices* you make. And *fate* can bring us to the devastating predicaments that our choices place us in, due to our *own* plans and decisions. But your *destiny* is the predetermined will of God for you. He has planned ahead of time, so that the proper events will *line-up* in your life, in order to *bring-about* in you the good benefits of His love, grace and mercy. Your *destiny* is in what God alone has *already* set-in order for you in eternity *past*. Since long before He even created this world into which you were born.

When we as mankind have difficulty discovering what God's *plans* for our present destiny is, it is because we tend to be so *busy* in fashioning the *works* of our *own* plans for ourselves. And in doing that, we fail to *rest* in God, so that we will get a *revelation* from God, of what the works of *His* plans of destiny for us are. And what they always *have* been, since before He created Earth.

> *"For we which have believed do enter into rest, as he said,*
> *As I have sworn in my wrath, if they shall enter into my rest:*
> *Although the works were finished from the foundation of the*
> *world."* **Hebrews 4:3** King James Version

Your *future* is what your *destiny* is. God has already stored it within your reach. It is *already* in your very *spirit* even *now*. You just have-to connect with the *Spirit* of the living God by *believing*! Then He will *reveal* His plan into your *mind*. Remember! You are a *Living Stone*! Created in the *image* of the high and merciful Lord God Almighty! You are an HEIR OF DESTINY! BELIEVE it! OWN it! LIVE it!

> *"May blessing (praise, laudation, and eulogy) be to the God and Father of*
> *our Lord Jesus Christ (the Messiah) Who has blessed us in Christ with*
> *every spiritual (given by the Holy Spirit) blessing in the heavenly realm!*
> *Even as [in His love] He chose us [actually picked us out for Himself*
> *as His own] in Christ before the foundation of the world, that we should*
> *be holy (consecrated and set apart for Him) and blameless in His sight,*
> *even above reproach, before Him in love. For He foreordained us*

(destined us, planned in love for us) to be adopted (revealed) as His own children through Jesus Christ, in accordance with the purpose of His will [because it pleased Him and was His kind intent]--- [So that we might be] to the praise and the commendation of His glorious grace (favor and mercy), which He so freely bestowed on us in the Beloved. In Him we have redemption (deliverance and salvation) through His blood, the remission (forgiveness) of our offenses (short-comings and trespasses), in accordance with the riches and the generosity of His gracious favor, Which He lavished upon us in every kind of wisdom and understanding (practical insight and prudence), Making known to us the mystery (secret) of His will (of His plan, of His purpose). [And it is this:] in accordance with His good pleasure (His merciful intention) which He had previously purposed and set forth in Him, [He planned] for the maturity of the times and the climax of the ages to unify all things and head them up and consummate them in Christ, [both] things in heaven and things on the earth. In Him we also were made [God's] heritage (portion) and we obtained an inheritance; for we had been foreordained (chosen and appointed beforehand) in accordance with His purpose, Who works out everything in agreement with the counsel and design of His [own] will." **Ephesians 1:3-11** Amplified Version

God has *always* had (and continues to have) a higher plan for us across the AGES of TIME. We have so *many* great and wonderful things that we can be proud of in our African heritage.

There is no nation or people upon the face of the earth that has not been minded toward war, conquest or slavery at some time in their history. Those characteristics are in all of mankind (either active or dormant at different times) as the open and exposed evidence of our fallen human nature since Adam. In God's plan and purposes for the AGES, we all; in our respective TIMES, rise above those characteristics and build great civilizations, as we become the HEIRS OF DESTINY.

But when we become strong as a nation, we must *not forget* God. We must *speak* peace, we must *seek* peace, and we must *keep* peace. For *all* of us.

HEIRS OF DESTINY

Searching My Heart

ABOUT

_____

WHAT SPECIAL MEANING *Part One* HAS FOR ME?

1. As a Black person, how do I see myself in relation to Today's world?

   _____
   _____

2. Do I believe it possible that God has a special purpose for giving me Life in this particular Time? __Yes __No   Here is the reason for my answer.

   _____
   _____

3. Faith is the means by which God empowers me to fulfill my Destiny. How can I begin to use my faith so that God will empower me for my Destiny?

   _____
   _____

4. In the plans of God, do I believe that these present Times are special for Black people? __Yes __No   Here is the reason for my answer.

   _____
   _____

5. What do I believe *Love* means to God? _____
   _____

6. What do I believe *Peace* means to God? _____
   _____

7. Can I *Personally* begin to have a heart to *Love* everyone, in *Peace*? _____

Part Two

GOD'S ORDERLY TRANSITION OF THE AGES

According as in the Heavens God has ordained the Dispensation in which certain peoples and nations will each lead, so too does He bring-about the Destinies of men in their Times upon the Earth, so that it is God Himself who performs His Plan through every nation of man that lives here

GLORY IN THE HEAVENS
YOUR TIMES, MY TIMES, OUR TIMES

When we read verses in the Bible about God's wondrous power and glory that He has placed in the Heavens above us, we should be awestruck. What we see in the Heavens tells us that God is perfecting His glorious works here upon the Earth:

> *"The heavens declare the glory of God; the skies proclaim the work of his hands. Day after day they pour forth speech; night after night they display knowledge. There is no speech or language where their voice is not heard. Their voice goes out into all the earth, their words to the ends of the world. In the heavens he has pitched a tent for the sun, which is like a bridegroom coming forth from his pavilion, like a champion rejoicing to run his course. It rises at one end of the heavens and makes its circuit to the other; nothing is hidden from its heat. The law of the LORD is perfect, reviving the soul. The statutes of the LORD are trustworthy, making wise the simple."* **Psalm 19:1-7** New International Version

It is in reading such verses as these, about the Heavens, that we begin to receive from God a picture revealed into our own spirit and soul. It is a picture that instills hope and inspires us to certain *awe* in God and His *majesty*. Such verses as these are God's way of directing us to believe in the fulfillment of great accomplishments. No matter how helpless hopeless weak small or insignificant we may have seen ourselves to be before this word of God became alive and relevant in us, its affects upon us should be nothing short of glorious and life-changing:

vs :1a *"The heavens declare the glory of God..."*

To *declare* something means to announce it openly; to show it or reveal it. There is nothing more open, revealing and visible to us who are here upon the Earth, than the heavenly skies that are above us. And *Psalm 19:1a* says that these visible heavenly skies that are above us are announcing and revealing openly to us the *glory* of God. For those nations of men and women who are God's chosen people in a particular AGE, God's **glory**; as it is understood in the scripture, is two things for them: [1] **light** [ie **illumination of the spirit and soul that is within them as God's chosen people**], and: [2] **blessing** [ie **enablement, spiritual ability, supply and provision for them as God's chosen people**]. In other words, God's chosen people in their TIMES are to be heavy [weighted-down and well endowed] with the *light* and *blessings* of God's *spiritual abilities*, and, with God's *supply and provision*.

Both of these: [1] *light* and [2] *blessing*, is God's *glory* being fulfilled within all of the people who are spiritual ISRAEL in the TIMES and DISPENSATIONS of their particular AGE.

Included with God's glorious declaration that is seen in the heavens, there is also this: **vs :1b** *".....the skies proclaim the work of his hands."*

PROCLAIM: To *proclaim* something is not much different than to *declare* it. They both mean to *announce openly*. The difference is, to *proclaim* something means that the announcement is an *official* one [ie someone having *authority* has issued a *proclamation*]. The TIMES will have *arrived*, for those peoples who are to become the HEIRS OF DESTINY. The *proclamation* in *'the skies'* has great meaning for them, with regards to their *'work'* here upon the Earth. God; in His word, makes it quite plain that He has provided great means of assistance for His HEIRS: *"But to which of the angels has He ever said, Sit at my right hand, until I make your enemies a footstool for your feet? Are they* (the angels) *not all ministering spirits, sent out to render service for the sake of those who will inherit salvation?"*

Hebrews 1:13-14 New American Standard Version

If we are to get a really good and clear understanding of Psalm 19 **vs :1b**, it would be this: 'the skies make the official announcement from God, that, the times for the new work of his hands is at its beginning upon the earth.'

<u>WORK</u> and <u>HANDS</u>: In this scripture, *'work'* is the accomplishments, manifestation and completion of certain acts upon the Earth that are *brought-to-pass* by God Himself. Since it is true that God is a *Spirit*, then, it is *we* who are His Heirs upon the *physical* Earth that also become His *'hands'*. God accomplishes the manifestation and completion of His *'work'* upon the Earth by personally guiding His chosen people [*spiritual* Israel] in order that they will fulfill His purposes here. That is why God empowers the peoples of spiritual Israel, each one, on an individual and *personal* level. He empowers them with the *light* and *blessing* of His *'glory'*; in their TIMES and DISPENSATIONS of a particular AGE upon Earth, so that He may manifest His *'work'* through them, as they become His *'hands'*.

Again, to *proclaim* means to make an announcement that is <u>official</u>. Only God can produce such <u>official</u> proclamation that can be seen in the *skies*. This is God's official announcement that tells the entire Earth that an AGE has arrived in which there will be TIMES and DISPENSATIONS that He will uniquely *bless* certain peoples of the Earth. Psalm 19:2-7 completes this account that God has written for us: <u>*Verses 2-4a*</u> tells us that day after day, and night after night God is (from within the heavens) speaking to His HEIRS OF DESTINY who are located worldwide. He speaks to each of them in their own language; giving knowledge to them of His plans and purposes for them and for the Earth, no matter where they may be living.

<u>*Verses 4b-7*</u> tells us also that God has set His certain boundaries for the Sun. So the Sun may traverse its circuit, moving across the heavens. And it touches every chosen Heir, to have its beneficial spiritual effect upon them, no matter how secluded and remote may be the place of the Heir's dwelling. According to these scriptures, it is in the heavens that God keeps *perfect* the operations of this spiritual law of His. So that, in their AGE and TIMES, the souls of His Heirs will become awakened. God does this because His statutes are ever trustworthy which He has set in order to make even the least and most simple Heir to become wise.

God has *handed-down* to us many, many scriptures such as Psalm 19, in order to explain how His system of heavenly bodies which He has placed in the skies fulfill their purposes. Such purposes as: announcing, communicating with, glorifying, empowering and blessing His chosen people, the HEIRS OF DESTINY.

But then, as we actually *look-up into* the heavens of Earth's skies, we are beholding literally the *manifest creation* of God. We are seeing God's representation of the invisible *spiritual*, as He is displaying it in that which appears above us as being the visible *natural*. And, like a living tapestry that is being woven with a multi-colored array of magnificent light, God is weaving the colors together in the heavens right before our eyes. He is weaving together the *light* and *blessing* of His glorious *events* of the AGE, for the benefit of us who are His Heirs here upon the earth.

It is in the *visible* heavens that are above *us* that God portrays for us what His *eternal* realms that are *above* the visible heavens must be like. Portraying for us, what His glory and great goodness that are in the heavens actually means for all of us here upon earth. And, He is portraying for us, what His glory and great goodness will *continue* to mean for us *all*; throughout all of the AGES, TIMES and DISPENSATIONS of MANKIND: *"But Israel shall be saved in the LORD with an everlasting salvation: ye shall not be ashamed nor confounded world without end."* **Isaiah 45:17** King James Version

In other words, God will always and forever continue to save *Israel*. He will never forsake (or stop saving) Israel, no matter who Israel might *be* at a given TIME in His plans for this world! The word *Israel* is a transitory title of designation, and is not a word that is intended to designate for *all time* any *one* specific ethnic group of people. The *word* (Israel) means: 'to rule as God' (or, more succinctly) 'to rule <u>with</u> God'. It is a word that is in direct reference to: who the particular or peculiar people are, that God Himself is working in and through at a given TIME in the AGES, in order to fulfill (by them) His holy purposes and plans for *all* of MANKIND and for Earth as a whole: *"But Israel shall be saved in the LORD with an everlasting salvation: ye shall not be ashamed nor confounded world without end."*

MAN and his relation to the AGES. God says more in the Bible regarding this subject than many of us care to take the time to read-about and to meditate upon. The *heavens* really *does* declare the *glory* of God. However, our human species seems to concern itself more with what is taking-place right here around us upon this Earth that God has created for us.

Focusing our attention on the things of the earth is normal. It is right, and it is our responsibility. Yet, even though we agree with this as being a normal and right responsibility entrusted to us from God, we see also that we tend to miss the bigger picture that God intends us to see. This *bigger picture* is one that has also been created by God just as our earth has. And God has *created* this bigger picture in the *heavens* above us. He has placed this bigger picture *directly above* us for the purposes of declaring His *glory* to us, and to all the rest of His Created Cosmos.

We as Man living upon our world is kind of like *us* (as mankind) being a colony of *ants*. Our immediate world is very tiny, and we (like the ant) do not seem to make very much about that. We just simply, do not pay very much attention to anything other than our own tiny world. But the creation *above* every ant colony is a whole other *much larger* world, with its *causes*, *effects*, and its *unique reality*.

It is no different with us humans. We condition ourselves to keep our gaze and purposes squarely focused on the events and activities of the immediate and finite world that is *before* us. While at the same time, with *us* (just as with the *ant* colony) a series of far *greater* and more *infinite* realities are unfolding right *above* us. And the *events* of these realities are forever taking-place in God's larger creation of the *heavens*. For us humans it is to the *heavens* that are right *above* us that we must pay more attention. They tell us of the AGES and DISPENSATIONS and TIMES that God has ordained for Man: *"NOW WHEN Jesus was born in Bethlehem of Judaea in the days of Herod the king, behold, there came wise men from the east to Jerusalem, Saying, Where is he that is born king of the Jews? For we have seen his star in the east, and are come to worship him."*

Matthew 2:1-2 King James Version

The creation account gives us a lot of important and meaningful information in regards to this *governance* of God's heavens over the Earth: *"IN THE beginning God created the heavens and the earth. The earth was formless and void, and darkness was over the surface of the deep, and the Spirit of God was moving over the surface of the waters. Then God said 'Let there be light'; and there was light. God saw that the light was good, and God separated the light from the darkness. God called the light day, and the darkness He called night. And there was evening and there was morning, one day. Then God said, 'Let there be an expanse in the midst of the waters, and let it separate the waters from the waters'. God made the expanse, and separated the waters which were below the expanse from the waters which were above the expanse; and it was so. God called the expanse heaven. And there was evening and there was morning, a second day. Then God said 'Let the waters below the heavens be gathered into one place, and let the dry land appear'; and it was so. God called the dry land earth, and the gathering of the waters He called seas; and God saw that it was good……..Then God said, 'Let there be lights in the expanse of the heavens to separate the day from the night, and let them be for signs and for seasons and for days and years; and let them be for lights in the expanse of the heavens to give light on the earth'; and it was so. God made the two great lights, the greater light to govern the day, and the lesser light to govern the night; He made the stars also. God placed them in the expanse of the heavens to give light on the earth, and to govern the day and the night, and to separate the light from the darkness; and God saw that it was good."*
Genesis 1:1-10; 14-18 New American Standard Version

According to this scripture the Bible is saying that our *days* and *nights* are *'governed'* [ruled, overseen, supervised] by the sun, the moon, and the stars. On a more practical level, this scripture is telling us that our wise, merciful and loving creator and God has set in His heavens above the earth an amazing mechanism that *cannot* be changed or controlled by any manner of our *human* intervention.

This amazing mechanism is the heavenly *clock* that has been created by God. God's eternal purpose for this clock is that it will effectively bring-about the *orderly passing of TIME* for all the AGES of Man. And it is *in* these AGES and TIMES of Man upon the earth, that God Himself pours into the hearts and minds of the men and nations of our world His pre-ordained *Destinies* for us. And then God *fulfills* HIS destiny *by* us, as He

Himself *brings-to pass* those things which He has already decreed for us since before we were born.

> *"From one man he made every nation of men, that they should inhabit the whole earth; and he **determined the times set for them** and the exact places where they should live. God did this so that men would seek him and perhaps reach out for him and find him, though he is not far from each one on us. For in him we live and move and have our being..."* **Acts 17:26-28**   New International Version   **bold text mine**

As we look [in the Bible] at periods of *TIME* in terms of the *AGES*, we come upon a treasure chest of most valuable information. Before we even take a look at a timetable concerning God's AGES for Man, let us first review a few Bible verses that speaks to us *clearly* about the AGES:

> *"For inquire, I pray thee, of the **former AGE**, and prepare thyself to the search of **their fathers**: (For we are but of yesterday, and know nothing, because our days upon earth are a shadow:)"*
> **Job 8:8-9**   King James Version   **bold text mine**

> *"But God, who is rich in mercy, for his great love wherewith he loved us, Even when we were dead in sins, hath quickened us together with Christ, (by grace ye are saved;) And hath raised us up together, and made us sit together in heavenly places in Christ Jesus: that in the **AGES to come** he might show the exceeding riches of his grace in his kindness toward us through Christ Jesus."*
> **Ephesians 2:4-7**   King James Version   **bold text mine**

> *"If ye have heard of the **dispensation** of the grace of God which is given to me to you-ward: How that by **revelation** he made known unto me the mystery; (as I wrote afore in few words, Whereby, when ye read, ye may understand my knowledge in the mystery of Christ) Which in **other AGES** was **not made known** unto the sons of men, as it is now **revealed** unto his holy apostles and prophets by the **Spirit**; That the Gentiles should be fellow**heirs**, and of the same body, and partakers of his promise in Christ by the gospel."*
> **Ephesians 3:2-6; 19-21**   King James Version   **bold text mine**

> *"Whereof I am made a minister, according to the **dispensation** of God which is given to me for you, to fulfill the word of God, Even the mystery which hath been **hid from AGES** and from generations, but now is made **manifest to** his saints: To whom God would **make known** what is the riches of the glory of this mystery among the Gentiles; which is Christ **in** you, the hope of **glory**."* **Colossians 1:25-27** King James Version **bold text mine**

Dispensation is a word that [from the biblical standpoint] simply means: a particular period of time in which God gives a particular assignment of stewardship (that includes the idea of provision and authority, with responsibility) to a particular person or group of people in order that God will fulfill His specific purpose and plan through them.

In every Dispensation God also enters a Covenant with those persons whom He charges as stewards. In the Covenant God states what His expectations *are* from those whom He has pre-ordained. God also makes *sure and certain promises* (which He keeps and fulfills) to His Covenant person or group of people.

Bible scholars vary greatly as to their interpretation of how many Dispensations and Covenants there are as seen in the scriptures. This inability to agree (on the part of the scholars) is nothing new in our world.

The Dispensations of God in regards to His AGES and TIMES for Man will never cease as long as our world Earth continues to exist. We looked-at this earlier in Isaiah 45:17 *"But **Israel** shall be saved in the LORD with an **everlasting** salvation; ye shall not be ashamed nor confounded **world without end**."*

In other words, we must find it within ourselves to believe and try to understand, that God's deeper truths is what is meant when we read such scriptures as **Hebrews 4:12-13** *"For the word of God is living and active and sharper than any two-edged sword, and piercing as far as the division of soul and spirit, of both joint and marrow, and able to judge the thoughts and intentions of the heart. And there is no creature hidden from His sight, but all things are open and laid bare to the eyes of Him with whom we have to do."*

To put it simply, the *word* of God is *living* and *active*. This means that the AGES, DISPENSATIONS and TIMES that God Himself has set for His Covenant with Man, each in their order, did not (and does not) come to an end with the end of the scriptures; or with the last verse that is written in the Bible: *"For this is the covenant that I will make with the house of Israel after those days, saith the Lord; I will put my laws into their mind, and write them in their hearts: and I will be to them a God, and they shall be to me a people."* **Hebrews 8:13** King James Version

We as humanity are *still* yet living our destinies under the guiding hand of God, even as Earth continues ever to exist: *"world without end"* **Isaiah 45:17**. God is *still* entering His Covenant with men in His DISPENSATIONS and TIMES for them throughout the AGES. YOU and I are alive *Now*! So *that* means *Now* is God's DISPENSATION and TIMES for His COVENANT with US!

DISPENSATIONS and DESTINIES
GOD'S GREAT CLOCK IN THE HEAVENS

To everything there is a season, and a <u>TIME</u> for every matter or purpose under heaven…He has made everything beautiful <u>IN ITS TIME</u>. He also has <u>PLANTED ETERNITY IN MEN'S HEARTS AND MINDS</u> [a divinely implanted sense of a purpose working through the <u>AGES</u> which nothing under the sun but God alone can satisfy], yet so that men cannot find out what God has done from the beginning to the end.

Those are not *my* words. Those are the words of King Solomon, written over three thousand years ago as recorded in Ecclesiastes 3 vs1 and 11 in the Amplified version of the Bible. They are words that give to us a sense that God has planned everything in advance for us according to what are His good purposes throughout the AGES. We are to fulfill these good purposes under the guiding *Spirit* of God within a set TIME that He Himself has ordained for each of us. The Bible also gives to us a good lesson about God's time-frame for an AGE. This gives us at-least a cursory understanding of the predestined TIMES and DISPENSATIONS for Man, according to the purposes of God in a certain AGE.

BEFORE WE REVIEW THE BIBLE AGES IT IS OF VITAL IMPORTANCE THAT I CAUTION YOU:

It is to God's own purposes that He has set in order the TIMES and DISPENSATIONS of Man. God alone has purposed that throughout the AGES of Man it is He himself who intervenes directly with men in a personal relationship that is made possible through salvation and the new birth. Salvation and the new birth have been extended to all of Mankind through the sacrificial death (on the Cross) of Jesus Christ the Son of God. He came into this world to pay the price (with His own blood) for our sin. By His crucifixion, resurrection and ascension; and, His sending the Holy Spirit into this world, we each can enjoy the fruitful life of having a personal relationship with God the Father, God the Son and God the Holy Spirit. **No astrology chart, palm reading, se'ance or any other such contrivance which Mankind may devise will ever please God. God detests all such things, referring to them as witchcraft, because He Himself; being our Creator, desires to have a personal relationship with each of us, so that He will guide us into and through the Destiny that He has *Pre*-destined for each of us from the foundation of the world.** It is for the passing-of AGES and DISPENSATIONS that God has set His glory in the *visible heavens* and *skies* that are above us. God has done this so that *at-least* we might know the TIMES in which our generations are to [as the scripture says] *SEEK HIM, although He is not far from every one of us, because it is IN HIM that we live and move, and have our *Being*.   *
Acts 17:27-28

THE AGES
A SPECIAL NOTE OF INTRODUCTION

As we look at 2000 to 2050 years periods of TIME in relation to the Bible. We should be careful to observe those periods of TIME in their relation to biblical persons and events. And as we do, God then begins to reveal to us a universal pattern that He has set in order. God uses this *universal order* within the Heavens and Skies that are above us so that He might raise-up (in our TIMES) the various Nations and Tribes and Peoples of the Earth.

God Himself doesn't need this *order in the heavens* to empower Him in His purposes of ruling us. But rather, God has set this order in the heavens and skies for *our* visible benefit. It is for His glory. So that *we* might know what is the AGE and the TIMES in which He has uniquely prepared *us* for our Destiny. So that we might know the TIMES in which we should be seeking the Lord Jesus Christ with all our heart.

When we connect this TIME of our *present* generation with the pattern that God is revealing to us in the Holy Bible, we begin to get a *picture* of what God wants us to *see*. It is a picture that His *order in the heavens* is showing to us right now.

We today are to *receive* this clear picture from God. It is a picture that is unmistakable regarding this *present* TIME of *our* generation. If we are going to receive this picture, we must first look to the AGES and the TIMES as we see them in the Holy Scriptures. They are the AGES and TIMES in which certain persons of the Bible lived. And, we must also see certain Bible *events* in their relation to a given AGE in which these events occurred under the guiding hand of God.

Finally, we who are the Black people must completely surrender ourselves to Christ in these amazing TIMES of DESTINY for *our* generation. God has set the *heavens* in order. He has a unique and special *purpose* for us *now* to become His Children of Destiny, ISRAEL [to Rule with God] as the people of His *calling*.

God's Heavenly Clock For The Ages

| Gemini | Taurus | Aries | Pisces | Aquarius | Capricorn |

Earlier than c 2000 B.C. *c 2000 B.C - c A.D. 1* *c A.D. 1 – c A.D. 2050*
                                                      Jesus Christ is Born

| Sagittarius | Scorpio | Libra | Virgo | Leo | Cancer |

Africa: Earlier than *c 2000* B.C.   The Age of Taurus

Genesis 1:1-11:32

- The CREATION account [God Creates the Heaven and the Earth]
- God gives ADAM [and MAN] DOMINION [rule] over the Earth
- God institutes MARRIAGE
- The FALL of MAN, and God's PROMISE of REDEMPTION
- MAN is EXPELLED from EDEN [Migrations / Exoduses begin]
- The Birth of CAIN, ABEL, SETH
- The first MURDER is committed
- The birth of NOAH [SHEM, HAM, JAPHETH]
- ANTEDILUVIAN CIVILIZATION [all the inhabitants of the world were one race, and all spoke the same language *cf Genesis 11:1-8*]
- The FLOOD
- Noah's sons, grandsons and civilizations *after* the FLOOD:

    SHEM: *Elam, Asshur, Arpachshad, Lud, Aram*

    HAM: *Cush, Mizraim, Put, Canaan*

    JAPHETH: *Gomer, Magog, Madai, Javan. Tubal, Meshech, Tiras*

- MAN attempts to build a tower [at Babel] into the Heavens
- God CONFOUNDS [confuses] Man's LANGUAGE and SCATTERS Man over the EARTH [further Migrations / Exoduses take place]
- ABRAHAM takes his wife SARAI and leaves the land of UR of the CHALDEES with TERAH his father.

AFRICA: c 2000 B.C. until about A.D. 1   The AGE of ARIES

GENESIS 12:1 – MALACHI 4:6
- From ABRAHAM [ISAAC, JACOB] to MOSES, to the KINGS and PROPHETS
- *PROPHECIES* increase about God's Son [JESUS CHRIST] coming to our world Earth.

*AFRICA: c A.D. 1 until about A.D. 2050   The AGE of PISCES

*[After World War II certain regions of Africa were changed in geographic designation to become referred to as the Middle East]

MATTHEW 1:1–JUDE 25   [The Book of The REVELATION reflects AGES *Past, Present* and *Future*]

- CHRIST the SAVIOR is born on Earth. In the TIMES of JESUS CHRIST the first symbol for the Christian Faith was the symbol of the FISH, representing the AGE of PISCES, the age of spiritual liberation and of freedom. This present year is A.D. 2014. We are *about* 2014 years forward since Christ's birth. But upon our world Earth; although *our* generation is at the *END* of the AGE, we are still in the AGE of PISCES.
- God's SALVATION is extended to *ALL* peoples of the Earth, so that God's purposes of LOVE, PEACE and GOOD WILL can further *cleanse* and *condition* the Heart and Soul of *FALLEN MAN*.
- The *GOSPEL* [God's Good News of spiritual Liberation, for men and women to become His Children, thereby fulfilling their *personal* and *corporate* DESTINY] is to be preached throughout the World, and offered to all Nations, Tribes and Peoples of the Earth.

Ephesians 2:4-10
"But because of his great love for us, God, who is rich in mercy, made us alive with Christ even when we were dead in transgressions---it is by grace you have been saved. And God raised us up with Christ and seated us with him in the heavenly realms in Christ Jesus, in order that in the **coming ages** *he might show the incomparable riches of his grace, expressed in his kindness to us in Christ Jesus. For it is by grace you have been saved, through faith---and this not from yourselves, it is the gift of God---not*

*by works, so that no one can boast. For we are God's workmanship, created in Christ Jesus to do good works, which God **prepared in advance** for us to do."* New International Version

The AGE of AQUARIUS BEGINS AT *about*: A.D. 2050

This will be the AGE in which God's universal *love* will influence the hearts and minds of Mankind, so that there will be greater opportunities for *peace* and a greater longing for unity among us. The results of the *love* and *peace* of God being accepted by Mankind, is that we (as a whole) will surrender our hearts to become filled with God's purposes for our entire species collectively. Then is when we will begin to truly reach the pinnacles of greatness for which God has created us. God will welcome Earth and Mankind into the greater and larger *creation* that is His Kingdom. Mankind will then experience exponential advances in all such areas of human civilization as *food production, technology, housing, travel conveyances,* and a transformed *system of exchange* for facilitating the obtaining of *goods and services* by and for everyone. Our world's present *market economy* (in all of its facets) is not a *just* means that speaks *honor* and *fair equity* to the masses. It is not a system built upon *righteousness*. It is not a system that would *please* or *glorify* God. It is a system that perpetuates great disparity between the *wealthy* and the *poor*: *"For the love of money is the root of all sorts of evil, and some by longing for it have wandered away from the faith and pierced themselves with many griefs."* **1 Timothy 6:10** New American Standard Version

Sadly, this mentality is prevalent in much of the religious-minded of today: *"If anyone teaches false doctrines and does not agree to the sound instruction of our Lord Jesus Christ and to godly teaching, he is conceited and understands nothing. He has an unhealthy interest in controversies and quarrels about words that result in envy, strife, malicious talk, evil suspicions and constant friction between men of corrupt mind, who have been robbed of the truth and who think that godliness is a means to financial gain."* **1 Timothy 6:3-5** New International Version

Heirs To The Heavens
Breaking The Cycle Of Uncertainty, Doubt and Frustration

Our present generation living right now upon the Earth is the generation in which God *even now* begins to shine His glorious *light* into our heart, spirit and soul. We are in the *early dawn* of God's new day *arising*. As God's new day sun *arises* on the horizon, we are just now catching the first rays of its *glow*, and the first glimpse of its rising *light* as it begins to shatter the darkness of what has been for us a long, long night. Let us not shield ourselves from the *light*. Let us bask in its *warmth* as it *declares* to us the Kingdom of Heaven, to the *glory* of God.

And most especially, if we as Black men, women and youths are to glorify God in our *hearts* as He is being glorified in the *heavens* above us, then, *we* must make some changes. The choices that we make and commit ourselves to must honor His *purposes* in these Times that are ours. There is absolutely no way around it. A genuine *love* for *all* of mankind, and a genuine *peace* (in our hearts) toward all *people*, MUST be the *way of life* for us.

In the Kingdom of the Heavens, God has set an *inheritance* for you. And that inheritance is the provision of God being extended to you, so that you may fulfill your Destiny. God makes this quite plain for us as we read Ephesians 1:3, 11 where the Word of God says: *"Blessed be the God and Father of our Lord Jesus Christ, who has blessed us with every spiritual blessing in the heavenly places in Christ.....also we have obtained an inheritance, having been predestined according to His purpose who works all things after the counsel of His will."* New American Standard Version

Identifying Your Heavenly Inheritance

Definitions:
1) IDENTIFY: a. 'to make a thing identical with something else'
   b. 'to connect with (or associate closely) with something'
   c. 'to know the identity of (or recognize) something'

2) IDENTITY CRISIS: *'the state of being uncertain of oneself regarding character, background, life-goals, reason for being etc'*

Before you can identify your *inheritance* that is in *heaven*, first the LIFE that is within you must identify with God our *Father* who is in heaven. It is He who has placed your inheritance there in heaven *for* you! In order that the LIFE within you will find its way to God our Father who is in heaven you must **begin** by identifying with Christ as the Son of God. In other words, you become *saved*, you have accepted God's salvation that He has (through Christ) extended to you. It is Christ who will then ***bring you*** to the Father, so that you may begin fulfilling your Destiny according to the Father's pre-ordained *will* and *purposes* for you. Jesus Christ makes this quite clear for us when He says in John 14:6 *"I am the way, the truth, and the life: no man comes unto the Father, but by me."*

Now, when you have become *saved* God then begins preparing you to fulfill His *purposes* for this personal relationship that you have entered into with Him. In essence the personal relationship that you have with God proceeds like this:

God *counsels* the LIFE that is within you and it grows-up into a spiritual *union* with Him. He does this within you in order to *bring-to-pass* His pre-determined *will* for having *given* you LIFE in the first place. In other words, you begin to *identify* with God our Father who is in Heaven.

The apostle Paul in his letter to the Ephesians gives to us some very priceless information with regards to the glorious *spiritual inheritance* that we receive from God during the process by which our Father in heaven *matures* the LIFE that is within us. Paul is communicating with the Ephesians concerning his prayers for them:

"I keep asking that the God of our Lord Jesus Christ, the glorious Father, may give you the spirit of wisdom and revelation, so that you may know him better. I pray also that the eyes of your heart may be enlightened in order that you may know the hope to which he has called you, the riches of his glorious inheritance in the saints, and his incomparably great power for us who believe, that power is like the working of his mighty strength."

Ephesians 1:17-19 New International Version

AN OPEN–BIBLE EXPOSITORY OF EPHESIANS 1:17-19

Ephesians 1:17
In this vs Paul begins to share with the church what it is that he is praying to God that we will *receive* from God: *"the spirit of wisdom and revelation, so that you may know him better."* This *'spirit of wisdom and revelation'* is how God fulfills His *purposes* in us, and how He brings-to-pass His predetermined *will* for the LIFE that He has *given* to us because we are His creation:

> Point: 1) God *gives* to us the *spirit* of: wisdom and revelation
> 2) So that we may *mature* spiritually into: knowing Him better

This is why Jesus Christ tells us in **John 10:15** *"As the Father knows me, even so know I the Father; and I lay down my life for the sheep"*. Why has Jesus Christ laid down His life for the sheep? So the sheep *also* can *personally know* the Father. And why do we want to personally know the Father? *Ephesians 1:18* Tells us why!

"that the eyes of your heart may be enlightened in order that you may know the hope to which he has called you, the riches of his glorious inheritance in the saints."

> Point: 1) For you to *receive* increased *personal* understanding and enlightenment *in your heart* into things that are *spiritual*
> 2) So that you can begin to *know* what the Father's *calling* is, for the LIFE that is within you
> 3) And in knowing, you will begin to have inside you a sense of HOPE
> 4) That you will become *awakened* to the *riches* of God's *light* and *blessing* that He has placed *inside* you, which is His *inheritance* to you

All of this inheritance and light and blessing and hope taking place inside us means very little. Until we receive POWER from GOD. We will need God's power so that through us, He will fulfill the works which He is proclaiming for these our TIMES.

In our text (through the words of the apostle Paul) God assures us that His own power as God, comes to us *directly* and *personally*. That power comes to us with its fullness of God's mighty strength. A mighty strength that we will need, in order that God's whole plan and purpose of spiritual maturity that He has predetermined for each of us will become a reality.

Ephesians 1:19
"and his incomparably great power for us who believe, that power is like the working of his mighty strength"

> Point: 1) God purposefully directs His power to you when you are a believer
> 2) Because God has specific works that He has planned for the power of His Spirit to accomplish in you, and through you

Even while we were making sinful choices in our lives; choices that were keeping us from becoming aware of the presence of God's Spirit that is always here with us. While we were making those sinful choices that hindered us from becoming awakened and enlightened to the goodness of God, even then, God was having mercy upon us, watching over us.

God did this because He knew that we are His Heirs. And He knew the TIMES and days were coming in which we who are His Heirs would willingly (and gladly) surrender our selfish *will* to Him and cease from our rebellious ways. He knew that only then would we; in genuine sincerity, give back to Him (to use for His own glory) the LIFE that He has *given* to us, the LIFE that is within us.

These *now* are the TIMES and days for which God has saved us. These are the TIMES and days in which He is looking for us to surrender ourselves unto His loving care. And, He's looking for us to lead others to awaken to His presence for their own LIFE that is found in Him, according to His plans.

Searching My Heart

ABOUT
_____

THIS PRESENT WORLD AGE and ME

1. Do I just happen to be living in this present period of time, or did God bring me here *now* for a special purpose? If He did, what unique traits or abilities do I have?

   _____
   _____
   _____

2. Based upon my unique traits or abilities, what could some of God's special purposes be for my life, as I am living in this particular time?

   _____
   _____
   _____

3. If I do not already know some of God's special purposes for me here and now, how can I go-about discovering them from God?

   _____
   _____
   _____

4. What do I need to be doing now, in order to position myself spiritually for receiving revelation from God about His special purposes for my life?

   _____
   _____
   _____

Part Three

IN MY COMMUNITY

The candid reflections of a Black pastor: my community is a picture of depression, deprivation and deterioration, a perfect painting of man's failure, the perfect canvass upon which God paints with the colors of His glory

I believe that a part of God's great purpose in Christ for all people is that we each come into the knowledge of who we are as His creation. I believe also, that every person who comes into this knowledge of their true self begins a process of spiritual transformation. When you know who it is (in Christ) that you are it develops you (in your soul) to becoming a person of quality and credibility. It is this *knowing* that should then become reflected in your character.

It is not difficult to imagine how such things as urban blight and inner-city squalor will radically change, as many of us who are the people living in these communities choose to begin making a 180 degrees turn in our life-choices. Does this mean that persons living in communities with manicured lawns, winding driveways and three-car garages are more moral-minded than people living in inner-city communities? No! Sin is a matter of thought, choices and actions no matter what income level you may be at, the level of education you may have, or the parcel of ground upon which your house may be standing.

Regardless of whose doorstep we lay the fault at for the problems facing our inner-city communities, the fact of life now, for *all* of us as humanity is this: *We all are affected by the personal choices and decisions of each one of us.* And just because some of us may choose to believe that this is *not* true, will never change the fact that it *is* true. None of us can hide from what we must all experience together and overcome as humanity. We can no longer hide in the man-made doctrines of our religious beliefs. We can no longer hide under the pretentious mantles of our higher education. We can no longer hide beneath the thin pigmentation in the color of our skin. Neither can we hide any longer in the economic social structures of our high (or low) income brackets. God is now calling to each and every one of us: *'come-out, come-out wherever you are'!* It is the higher plans and purposes of God that now awaits us all.

Crime, violence and drug trafficking will quickly become gone from the streets of our inner-city communities; and our people will begin to flourish, when we as Black people decide to work together at raising the mindset and spirit of us all.
In all of our endeavors, our most valiant and committed efforts as Africans should be to the discovering of our great spiritual heritage that is founded (once and for all) in the *call* of the living God to us.

In these days we must refocus our minds. We must re-direct our purposes and intentions. Then will the perception within our spirit and soul become raised to unimaginable levels of clarity. Raised to those places in our life where the light of God's divine destiny in Christ for each of us will at-last become *revealed* in us.

Is it *possible*? Or, could it *be*? That God in His most Holy wisdom has set a purpose for these TIMES in the Destiny of men's lives. That, something which before has been unthinkable in the mind of most men is now beginning to take place. The next great wave of spiritual revolution, in which, God will reveal higher levels and dimensions of His Kingdom priorities into the soul of mankind. Could it be, that God is revealing these Kingdom priorities to us right now *in* those persons that He is *calling-to* right here in their *struggles* and *hardships* of inner-city hopelessness. Those very persons who are right now at this *present* time living in urban-blight, low esteem and demoralization. That sounds *just exactly* like God: *"Brothers, think of what you were when you were called. Not many of you were wise by human standards; not many were influential; not many were of noble birth. But God chose the foolish things of the world to shame the wise; God chose the weak things of the world to shame the strong. He chose the lowly things of this world and the despised things--and the things that are not---to nullify the things that are, so that no one may boast before him."* **1 Corinthians 1:26-29** New International Version

What is it that made our African ancestors so great a people in those by-gone eras thousands of years ago in antiquity? What did they have that we seem to be missing? What is it that we seem to have lost? They formed great communities, and even built great entire civilizations! Yet, we cannot seem to even bring a small neighborhood together for the good of all. Have we missed the message that the genetic marker God has placed in us has been transmitting to us? We are humans *Being*. Open your mind, open your heart, and begin to *Be*. We do that by getting in GOD: *"For in him we live and move and have our Being"* **Acts 17:28**

When we take a close look at what the apostle Paul is saying to us here we begin to make some phenomenal discoveries. The phrase *"...in him we live and move...."* is quite self-explanatory: 'it is in God that we have been given the ability to subsist, having breath, flowing blood and functioning limbs, organs and body parts so that we can live and move'. But then Paul (in Acts 17:28b) gives to us a word that is more *ethereal* in its meaning to us; more *celestial*, *other-worldly* and exceptionally *delicate* to our senses. Paul says in the second part of that verse: *"...and have our Being"*. The apostle just then has taken the verse to a higher spiritual level!

To have *'being'*, means to have cognitive abilities. It means having the ability to reason, to make decisions and choices. These are all things that are done on a *spiritual* level! To frame a *thought*, and then to intellectually carry-out the *mental* planning that is associated with making the *thought* become something that is manifest as *real* and *tangible*. What began as a thought became something that you can see, taste, touch, smell and hear with your physical senses. To *'have our being'* in *God* means that we are to *involve* God in all of our planning and implementing of the things that are associated with our LIFE here.

Having your *Being* in God is going-to impact your LIFE in three very important and meaningful ways:

> #1) It is going-to give to you; finally, a sense of *emotional deliverance* and release from the trials, hurts and mistaken choices of your *PAST*.

#2) It is going-to give to you the *assurance* that comes with having the spiritual empowerment that God inspires you with in your P*resent*.

#3) It is going-to give to you a *greater clarity* relating to the amazing plans that God has for you in your F*uture*.

What Having Our Being In God Can Achieve In Us

Since 1966 when I was about 22 years of age I have felt myself being curiously drawn by something that even now is still deep within my soul. That something which was continually drawing me was: a seemingly insatiable longing to learn whatever I could about the history and culture of the ancient Egyptians. This peculiar longing inside me became to me the very foundation and framework for a life-time of personal research and inquiry. And so, for the past nearly five decades of my life I have been mysteriously directed (with a most keen interest) to so many studies and writings pertaining to this amazing people of antiquity.

I grew-up in a family that has a very Baptist oriented church-active background that is rooted in the Christian faith. So I did not have the problem of possibly becoming side-tracked into the beliefs of a far distant religion that was rooted in an ancient past of which I had (and still have) much to learn.

There has never been any doubt in my mind that Jesus Christ only, is the one true way to salvation, to God the Father, and, to the new birth and eternal life.

But still, there was this---something----deep within the soul of me that was ever craving to be fed with knowledge concerning these ancient Black people. Over the years I've learned that they had a high sense of *spiritual* perception and high *moral* values. They also possessed unique and gifted talents and the undeniable ability to produce an awe-inspiring beauty that was woven into the very fabric of their religious culture, and, into the communities of their society and civilization.

Today, after having engaged myself in nearly fifty years of consistent and focused independent studies, I have no reservations about admitting that I am neither a scholar nor an authority on the subject of ancient Egypt and its peoples. Nor do I wish to be perceived as a person who vainly pre-supposes to represent himself as such. But, that having been said, this one thing I *do* know:

Many persons who in the past have been; and today are, the so-called scholars pertaining to matters of ancient Egypt and its people, have for centuries (whether intentionally or un-intentionally): either misread, misunderstood, misinterpreted, or misrepresented to the world; the remarkable truths concerning these highly gifted Black people, who were also highly skilled in arts, philosophy, mathematics, architecture, astronomy and other sciences. They had laws governing their civilizations. They were also a very spiritual and highly reverent people in their perception of God and in their worship.

Not *all* scholars of ancient Egyptian history have been disingenuous. There are those who have a deep desire to simply know (and share) the *truth*. And, it is for their honesty and integrity that we are truly thankful to God. Their sincerity and valor is meaningful to many Black people living in many communities today.

Christ Jesus is the Son of the living God, and the Savior of all mankind. Man's salvation is contingent upon his *believing* in Jesus Christ as our Savior and Lord, and then accepting Christ into our heart. Whoever asks Christ into their heart *will* become *born-again*, and will have access to God the Father, and to God the Holy Spirit. Then, with the proper discipleship, which involves biblical learning and spiritual nurturing, those persons who accept Christ will begin to enjoy the amazing LIFE of a *soul* that prospers.

Right now; we as Black men and women, should be shaping the thoughts and plans for our lives (and for the lives of our children and youths) around three main areas of *spiritual* interest pertaining to us and the communities in which we live. And when we really begin to *do* this, we will see God's intended *spiritual revolution* of Love, Peace and Faith begin to take-place in our grass-roots communities.

THREE PRIMARY SPIRITUAL AREAS AROUND WHICH WE MUST FOCUS IN OUR COMMUNITIES

1) We each have a Destiny, God *planned* it for us long before we were born

2) We each have a Spiritual Inheritance from God, *stored-up* in heavenly places for each of us, in Christ Jesus, so that we each can *fulfill* our Destiny here

3) We each have a Heritage here, a *bloodline* that dates all the way back to our ancient forefathers who *knew* God, and not a single one of us is inferior or just happens to be here; *wherever* here may be for each of us

BY MISSING GOD'S UNIQUE MESSAGE FOR US
WE RISK ALSO MISSING HIS UNIQUE ANOINTING FOR US

As a pastor for some thirty years now, I have discovered that one of the most difficult and challenging missions in the Black church is to openly (and in a relevant way) disciple our people into a better understanding of the message relating to our true heritage. The move to disciple our people into a better understanding of our true heritage as Africans should certainly be carried-on simultaneously with our Bible studies that disciple us into a spiritual *union* with Christ. There is absolutely no one who is more qualified to teach our history *to* us; or teach it *for* us, than *us*. I firmly believe that by familiarizing ourselves with the legacy of the illustrious *past* of our ancestral fathers and mothers we will also inspire our *present* Black generation to come into the fullness of reaching our own true potential and ability in God.

When Jesus Christ was preparing His disciples to go-out and witness God's truth to a world that had been living in darkness and ignorance, He makes a very powerful statement to them that we as Black men and women should take to heart about ourselves today in our present relationship with Him as our Lord: *"...there is nothing covered, that shall not be revealed; and hid, that shall not be known."*

Matthew 10:24 King James Version

In the verse we've just read Christ is saying to us for the sake of beginning our spiritual awakening today in our present generation: *'whatever spiritual truths that pertain to you becoming awakened unto your personal destiny; and receiving your personal anointing, these spiritual truths have not been kept hidden away **from** you, but rather they have been kept hidden away **for** you; to become revealed **only to you** in the **times** that are **yours**'*

The particular glory that God receives through the beauty of His Word is that His Word is alive and there is no *one* personal interpretation of it. No one can take the Word of God and make it mean for *everyone else* what *they* want it to mean for all of *time*. God awakens our *being* by the means that His Word is *alive* and *living* within us. The Word of God has a purpose. When we let it, the Word of God becomes *real* to us in ways that are very relevant to *our* times and generation, according as God has so purposed. And so God's Word actually *examines* us and conditions us for the work to which God has given LIFE to *our* generation: *"For the word of God is living and active. Sharper than any two-edged sword, it penetrates even to dividing soul and spirit, joints and marrow; it judges the thoughts and attitudes of the heart."*

Hebrews 4:12 New International Version

God has done this so that in every AGE, in every DISPENSATION, in the TIMES of every *chosen* generation; His Holy Word will have its unique and special *meaning* for those to whom God is *revealing* Himself, which are His HEIRS OF DESTINY.

When we as Black men and women surrender ourselves to God *in faith*, we will begin to enjoy a remarkable transformation taking-place within us; and, within our children and their children of our present generations. It is only as we surrender ourselves to God *in faith,* that we will be ready to receive the gift of God's *grace* in an increased *anointing* to us: *"Grace and peace be multiplied to you in the knowledge of God and of Jesus our Lord; seeing that His divine power has granted to us everything pertaining to life and godliness, through the true knowledge of Him who called us by His own glory and excellence. For by these He granted to us His precious and magnificent promises, so that by them you may become **partakers of the divine nature**, having escaped the corruption that is in the world by lust."* **2 Peter 1:2-4** New American Standard Version

Through His increased anointing to us God will use us for glorious achievements both now and in the future. God is doing this for purposes of continuing to further His Holy Kingdom that He is establishing here among us. The work that is to be accomplished in this our time and generations is for the good of *all* mankind according to the determinate *will* of God.

DRUG DEALERS and STREET-CREWS IN MY COMMUNITY

Drug-trafficking and those who take-part in it are destroying the *spiritual quality of LIFE* that God has created every person to experience by their personal relationship with Him through Christ. Drug-trafficking and drug-use is witchcraft and idolatry. They steal, kill and destroy an individual's spiritual ability to have their *'being'* in God in a personal way. To know God in a way that can be *experienced* in their very *soul*. Unless they who traffic in such witchcraft and idolatry repent, there is no human mind that can imagine how terrible God's eternal punishment and damnation is going-to be upon them for having caused or contributed to the violating and confusing of another person's *spirit* or *soul*.

And yet even in the midst of all this, there is this one *truth* that I am certain of. This truth continues to be a recurring source of hope within my soul, and it is the guiding principle behind the faith of my calling. And that one truth that I am still certain of is this: God has a *divine and eternal plan of destiny and purpose* for the people of these communities such as my community is. And most especially we who are this present generation, God desires that we come to know who we are as a people. *"Beloved, I pray that in all respects you may **prosper** and be in **good health**, just as your **soul prospers**. For I was very glad when brethren came and testified to your truth, that is, how you are **walking in truth**. I have **no greater joy** than this, to hear of my children walking in the truth."* **3 John 2-4** New American Standard Version

This community in which God has placed me is one whose DISPENSATION and TIME has come. God is ready to bless this community with a glorious transformation that includes blessing every person living here who has a desire for a better life. I have been blessed to see men and women become *delivered* from the strongholds of drug-addictions, and, then become saved. I've watched them grow spiritually, and many have moved-on to become leaders in the church. Some of them have become men and women who are now preaching and teaching God's truths with a love and compassion that is genuine and effective in transforming the lives of others. And yet in my community; still *now* even, there remains the drug-trafficking that continues to destroy in some people the great potential that God has *created* within them.

What makes any generation of people *honorable* is how they observe the laws, and keep the moral code of the civilization and culture in the TIMES which they find themselves living. But the thing that makes a generation *great*, and progresses them forward into God's *glorious future* for them, is when they re-discover the *Spirit of God* in that which gave to their ancestors and forefathers God's sense of *'Being'* regarding the *destiny*, *unity* and *purpose* that He has *pre-determined* for their LIFE here on Earth! Again, we must call to remembrance God's word to the prophet Jeremiah: *"For I know the thoughts that I think toward you, saith the LORD, thoughts of peace, and not of evil, to give you an expected end, Then shall ye call upon me, and ye shall go and pray unto me, and I will hearken unto you. And ye shall seek me, and find me, when ye shall search for me with all your heart."* **Jeremiah 29:11-13**

That is what will transform the individual, the family, the neighborhood, the community, the people, the tribe, the city, the nation and the world.

And so, this problem community that you've just read of, this is the community that I live in, this is my community! And, I know in my *heart*, that God has great plans for the future of my community. I know that there are still some problems in my community. But these can all be overcome with persistent purposeful patience, and with genuine and sincere (but disciplined) Christian *love*.

But also in my community, I believe that it is in the *knowing* of our distant and ancient Black heritage that will give to us God's enduring hope and encouragement to *excel*, and to be fruitful in life. And today, we; as the offspring of our ancient fathers, are to represent them with *dignity* and with a deep sense of commitment to those things that make *any* people great. Such things as: *faith, honor, duty, loyalty,* a commitment to *truth*, and above all, *Love* and *Peace*; having a sense of *holiness*, without which, as Hebrews 12:14 says: *"...no man shall see the Lord."*

We owe no less to this present generation before whom God has brought us into this world for a *witness*, we owe no *less* to them than to deliver to them, all that our heavenly Father has entrusted into our soul to be delivered unto them.

> *"Then shall the king say unto them on his right hand,*
> *Come, ye blessed of my Father, Inherit the kingdom*
> *prepared for you from the foundation of the world."*
> **Matthew 25:34**

Black man, Black woman, in these Times God has opened all the Heavens above to you. He has made the whole Earth available to you. What are you going-to do with yourself to benefit humanity in these Times? Will you be a catalyst for *love*, or for hate? A catalyst for *peace*, or for conflict? For *help*, or for hurt? *Healing*, or wounding? What are you going-to do with your *spiritual inheritance* so that you may benefit humanity in these Times?

Searching My Heart

ABOUT

_____

THE COMMUNITY WHERE I LIVE

1. What can I do to make the community where I live become a place of spiritual awakening and useful purpose?

   _____
   _____
   _____

2. If my community already has these qualities, what community can I adopt so that I can be helpful in elevating their potential toward spiritual awakening?

   _____
   _____
   _____

3. What are some things that I will need to do in my own life before I can begin to work with helping others to enter their spiritual quest for becoming aware that they are an Heir of God?

   _____
   _____
   _____

4. What do I need to do to get started in discovering my own potential as the Heir to this great spiritual legacy that I have been given from God?

   _____
   _____
   _____

Part Four

TO THE ELECT OF GOD

*What it means to be Black, Now, Chosen by God, and
living your life in the most amazing relationship of all Time*

In today's 21st Century civilization, unless you possess a pure *Love* for *all* of humanity you cannot and will not fulfill the purposes of God. This is the one characteristic displayed openly from within man that epitomizes the *ideal* of God's Holy purposes for us that we are called-upon to *aspire to* as His creation. Love! It is the very nature of God in the person or persons whom He has *chosen* to represent the manifestation of His own *living essence* being present with us in humanity here on Earth:

"Beloved, let us love one another, for love is from God; and everyone who loves is born of God and knows God. The one who does not love does not know God, for God is love. By this the love of God was manifested in us, that God has sent His only begotten Son into the world so that we might live through Him. In this is love, not that we loved God, but that He loved us and sent His Son to be the propitiation for our sins. Beloved, if God so loved us, we ought also to love one another. No one has seen God at any time; if we love one another, God abides in us, and His love is perfected in us. By this we know that we abide in Him and He in us, because He has given us of His Spirit." **1 John 4:7-13**
New American Standard version

Love is the hallmark of the *Elect* of God, and it is the identifying quality present within those who are the redeemed. Being the *Elect* of God, means that you have become officially *welcomed* and *oriented* by God Himself (and the holy angels) into the *spiritual union* that is associated with His *salvation* and *destiny* for you. It is while you are in this spiritual union with God and the holy angels associated with His destiny for you, that you will fulfill the *works* to which God has *predestined* you. Since *before* He had even *created* this world *or* you, by His own *determinate will* God had already prepared for this spiritual union with you, and for the works that you in *your* TIME would accomplish as a result of this union:

"For we which have believed do enter into rest, as he said, As I have sworn in my wrath, if they shall enter into my rest; although the works were finished from the foundation of the world."
Hebrews 4:3 King James Version

"But to which of the angels has He ever said, 'Sit at my right hand, until I make your enemies a footstool for your feet'? Are they not all ministering spirits, sent out to render service for the sake of those who will inherit salvation?" **Hebrews 1:13-14** New American Standard Version

God's ELECT: Any person or people whom God has specifically chosen to be in a special relationship with him. They are the vessels with whom God will enter into a unique covenant of blessing. During a certain AGE, DISPENSATION or period of TIME in which God has pre-determined that the person or people will become divinely led by Him; God will bring them to salvation and make His plan and purposes become known to them. God will show His great favor (grace) toward them, and He will display His favor to the rest of the world through them. God's special name in any given TIME for the person or persons who are His ELECT is: ISRAEL. The name Israel means: *to rule as God* (or) *to rule with God*. The Gentile is any person or persons who are not the ISRAEL persons of whose TIMES it is *to rule with God*.

The people who are the Israel of God are *always* called-together by God himself through angels or His prophets etc. They then begin to be led-forth by God as they are ushered *out* of a time that had been filled with either oppression or a particular hardship for them, in which time they most likely were also steeped in a mire of deep spiritual darkness. As the people of God are being led forth God begins His transformation of them by ushering them together *into* the TIME of the *dawning* of His *great glory* beginning to *rise* upon them and within them:

"ARISE, SHINE; for your light has come, And the glory of the LORD has risen upon you. For behold, darkness will cover the earth And deep darkness the peoples; But the LORD will rise upon you And His glory will appear upon you. Nations will come to your light, And kings to the brightness of your rising. Lift up your eyes round about and see; They all gather together, they come to you. Your sons

will come from afar, And your daughters will be carried in the arms. Then you will see and be radiant, And your heart will thrill and rejoice; Because the abundance of the sea will be turned to you, The wealth of the nations will come to you."

Isaiah 60:1-5 New American Standard Version

What is it here that God is saying nearly three thousand years ago to the people who were Israel in the 8th century B.C.? There are some very special things that God is saying to them through the prophet Isaiah. And; in saying it, God is encouraging His (then) chosen people to *awaken* unto the *times* of His *glory* for them while at the same time God is *instructing* them concerning what He is about to *do* with them as His *blessings* become manifest to them:

"ARISE, SHINE; for your light has come, And the glory of the LORD has risen upon you"
<u>What this verse is saying:</u> 'Get up, and choose to *come into the awareness* of your *Being*, because the time has arrived in which you will stand-out in your *brightness*, as you exhibit the magnificence of the light and blessings of my presence that has now become *raised unto its manifestation* upon you'.

<u>What this means to us today as God's Heirs of Destiny:</u> We as Black men and women each now in our present generation are to wake-up and make our personal decision to become serious about our relationship with God. And, we must allow God to transform us into the person of DESTINY that He has given us LIFE for becoming in this Present TIME.

"For behold darkness will cover the earth And deep darkness the peoples"
<u>What this verse is saying:</u> 'Look around you, the lack of spiritual light will extend over the whole earth. And also a deep void will exist over many people groups. This is because there will be extending far down to within the soul of these people a place where there is the *absence* of any *spiritual enlightenment*'.

<u>What this means for us today as God's Heirs of Destiny:</u> Search deeply into your hearts and minds as Black people in this present TIME, so that the love and knowledge of God will become revealed unto you along with the great wisdom of God. And hold-onto these things in your heart with the peace of God.

"But the LORD will arise upon you And His glory will appear upon you."
<u>What this verse is saying</u>:   'Nevertheless, God Himself will raise His *Being* into manifestation *upon you*, and His light and blessing will become visible to all, so that they will see the *presence* of God upon you'.

<u>What this means for us today as God's Heirs of Destiny</u>:   In spite of what is going-on in the world around you, God is going-to make known to the world that His glorious presence is with you as Black men and women. This does not in any way give to you a license to be rude, callous and insensitive. In fact, God expects the exact opposite from you. You represent the grace, love and mercy of God, if you cannot extend that grace love and mercy to every other human being, then, you yourself are not deserving of it.

"Nations will come to your light, And kings to the brightness of your rising."
<u>What this verse is saying</u>:   'Other people groups will come before you just to bask in the brightness of God's *presence* as He exhibits and displays His *glory* upon you. And great leaders; being among some of these people groups, will also come before you'.

<u>What this means for us today as God's Heirs of Destiny</u>:   One of the most difficult things for human-beings to do is to remain stayed and calm as their everyday existence begins to enter a period of time when they seem to receive more attention. They begin to plan their lives for the attention. Keep to the work of God that is at-hand, stay the course, there is something much more important to humanity here than getting attention from others. God is fulfilling His Divine and Holy Purposes. God's Kingdom business FIRST! SECOND! and ALWAYS!

"Lift up your eyes round about and see; They all gather together, they come to you."
<u>What this verse is saying</u>:   'Raise your eyes from their downward glance of hopelessness and look around you, the people all come together and assemble where you are, they are drawn to you'.

<u>What this means for us today as God's Heirs of Destiny</u>:   There is no time to feel distraught, or hopelessness and despair. Look around you, at your friends neighbors and loved-ones. What do you see? What kind of lives are they living? God has a high purpose for you in having the people become drawn to the light of His glory that has risen upon you. YOU must begin to make yourself available to God so that He can direct you in ways to have a good and positive effect upon the lives of others who are around you.

"Your sons will come from afar, And your daughters will be carried in the arms."
<u>What this verse is saying</u>:   'Your *kinsmen* in distant places will know in their spirit that this is the move of God, and they will make an effort to come to you in any way that they can, from wherever they are'.

<u>What this means for us today as God's Heirs of Destiny</u>:   Strengthen your personal resolve to become unified with those persons who are seeking the true purposes of God to become revealed into their life. The old paradigms of competing against one another must be done-away with. There must be new covenants of unity that exemplify the common-good and good-will for all. There must be community building, and especially with close-attention to establishing spiritually safe and progressive family models among us for ourselves and for our children.

"Then you will see and be radiant, And your heart will thrill and rejoice; Because the abundance of the sea will be turned to you, The wealth of the nations will come to you."
<u>What this verse is saying</u>:   'Then your eyes will be *opened* to what God is doing and your face will beam with *bright joy*, your heart also will be *jubilant*, because all of your people in the various nations will be with you in this *true spiritual awakening* and growth that God has for the nations'.

<u>What this means for us today as God's Heirs of Destiny</u>:   There is no person on our world who should miss-out on the remarkable things that God Himself is doing right now in the Black man and woman. But first and foremost the two of them must work together in a homogeneous relationship that is directed by God. The legacy of our

unification in spirit and soul that is *coming forth right now* into our Times is a legacy that is coming-down to us from God. Our world must begin to accept this truth that: this is God's plan for *our present generation* and for the good of our entire world. And when we do accept it, then will begin to take-place in our world an increasingly *reduced* sense of attention that currently is being paid to the bringing-about of social and civil persecutions upon some who are among us.

*"And ye shall hear of wars and rumors of wars; see that ye be not troubled; for all these things must come to pass, but the end is not yet. For nation shall rise against nation, and kingdom against kingdom; and there shall be famines, and pestilences, and earthquakes in various places. All these are the beginnings of sorrows……..And many false prophets shall rise, and shall deceive many. And because iniquity shall abound, the love of many shall [grow] cold. But he that shall endure unto the end, the same shall be saved. And this gospel of the kingdom shall be preached in all the world for a witness unto all nations; and then shall the end come……..For then shall be great tribulation, such as was not since the beginning of the world to this time, nor ever shall be. And except those days should be shortened, there should no flesh be saved; but for the **Elect's** sake those days shall be shortened. Then if any man shall say unto you, Lo, here is Christ, or there; believe it not. For there shall arise false christs, and false prophets, and shall show great signs and wonders; insomuch that, if it were possible, they shall deceive the very **Elect**……..And he shall send his angels with a great sound of a trumpet, and they shall gather together his **Elect** from the four winds, from one end of heaven to the other……..For as in the days that were before the flood they were eating and drinking, marrying and giving in marriage, until the day that Noah entered into the ark."* **Matthew 24:6-8…11-14…21-24…31…38** King James Version

*"Put on therefore, as the **Elect** of God, holy and beloved, tender mercies, kindness, humbleness of mind, meekness, longsuffering; Forbearing one another, and forgiving one another, if any man have a quarrel against any: even as Christ forgave you, so also do ye. And above all these things put on love, which is the bond of perfectness. And let the peace of God rule in your hearts, to the which also ye are called in one body; and be ye thankful. Let the word of Christ dwell in you richly in all wisdom; teaching and admonishing one another in psalms and hymns and spiritual songs, singing with grace in your hearts to the Lord. And whatsoever ye do in word or deed, do all in the name of the Lord Jesus, giving thanks to God and the Father by him."*
Colossians 3:12-17 King James Version

Finally, you are the heirs of these Times! So then, BE--- Heirs of Destiny!

The Author's Personal Reading Helps

Reference and Resources Relating To This Subject Matter

The AFRICAN ORIGIN OF CIVILIZATION, MYTH OR REALITY
                                                       Cheikh Anta Diop
Lawrence Hill Publishers

The AFRICANS WHO WROTE THE BIBLE
                         Nana Banchie Darkwah
Aduana Publishing

ANCIENT EGYPT THE LIGHT OF THE WORLD
                       Gerald Massey
Black Classic Press

BLACK GENESIS, THE PREHISTORIC ORIGINS OF ANCIENT EGYPT   Robert Bauval & Thomas Brophy
Bear & Company

The DESTRUCTION OF BLACK CIVILIZATION
                       Chancelor Williams
Third World Press

The EGYPTIAN BOOK OF THE DEAD
                       E. A. Wallis Budge
Dover Books

FOUNDATIONS FOR FAITH
                       Peter Toon
Crossway Books

The HOLY BIBLE *Versions: KJV, NASV, NIV*

The REAL MEANING OF THE ZODIAC
                       D. James Kennedy
Coral Ridge Ministries

The SIRIUS MYSTERY
                       Robert K G Temple
St. Martins Press